The Story of God and His People

The Day of the Lord

Second edition by

Beth Lantinga

First edition by

Arthur Tuls Jr.
Neal Bierling

CHRISTIAN SCHOOLS
INTERNATIONAL

CHRISTIAN SCHOOLS INTERNATIONAL
3350 East Paris Ave. SE
Grand Rapids, Michigan 49512-3054

Second Edition
© 1998 CHRISTIAN SCHOOLS INTERNATIONAL
Printed in the United States of America
All rights reserved

10 9 8 7 6 5 4 3

ISBN 0-87463-966-2

The development of *The Story of God and His People* was made possible with grants from Christian Schools International Foundation and Canadian Christian Education Foundation, Inc.

Photographs by Neal and Joel Bierling, Phoenix Data Systems.
Illustrations: Gustave Doré: 7, 13, 16, 17, 34, 40, 42, 79, 133, 142; The Granger Collection: 77, 165; SuperStock: 9, 26, 53, 147, 155, 174, 186; all other illustrations and maps by Teresa Wyngarden.

Contents

1 – – ➤ The Beginning of the Story

> **Bible Reference: Genesis 1–11**

What do you think of when you hear the word *story*? Do you think of curling up in a chair and reading the adventures of your favorite hero? Or sitting around the table on Thanksgiving Day and hearing familiar family tales?

Do you connect the word *story* with the Bible? The Bible is a story, too, with a setting, characters, themes, a plot, and a wonderful ending. It really happened. It's a true story that began in Eden, and it's not over yet. The end is still coming.

Characters and Setting

This year you will jump into the middle of the Old Testament story. We'll look at the story of God and his people from the reign of King Solomon, 965–928 B.C., to Jesus' birth and early life. The stories in *The Day of the Lord* take place in Palestine until God's people go into exile in Babylon.

You will hear the voice of God, the main character. He reveals his heart and mind through early prophets like Elisha and Elijah and later prophets like Jeremiah. The prophets represent God. The other characters represent all people in all times and places. You don't have to look far to find people who respond to God's call like King Hezekiah or, for that matter, like Queen Jezebel.

Themes

Throughout this year you will also encounter several themes and key

Mount Sinai.

ideas. They weave through the stories of Israel's and Judah's prophets and kings. The covenant that God made at Mount Sinai expressed his love for his people and described the way they ought to live. It was part of his plan to heal the break that sin created. If the people obeyed the covenant's requirements, God would bless them. If they disobeyed, they would meet disaster. This year you will see disobedient kings lead their people into disastrous judgment. The prophets often referred to the judgment that resulted from sin and disobedience as the day of the Lord.

But the day of the Lord also referred to a day of hope and mercy. The time was coming when God would shower his faithful, obedient people with great drops of blessing. Restoration and healing are key themes in the Old Testament. The story of Naaman's river cure reveals God's merciful desire to heal, and it shows God's mercy and love for Gentiles as well as Jews. Another sign of God's mercy is his unwillingness to give up on his people. Through the prophets' voices God constantly called his people back from their wandering ways. Over and over the prophets cried to the people, "I made you. I love you! Why won't you listen?" Some of the most beautiful signs of God's mercy are the prophecies pointing to the messiah. Jesus perfectly obeyed the covenant's requirements and became the perfect sacrifice. Watch for signs of the messiah.

Plot

Let's review where the conflict between good and evil first erupted.

"In the beginning God created the heavens and the earth." This is the opening sentence of the story. Genesis 1 goes on to tell us that there is one

God and he is the Creator. Everything else, including the human race, is part of the creation. God made people in his image—different from anything else in creation.

Genesis 3:8–9 suggests that God came to the garden to be with Adam and Eve. He wanted fellowship with them. Adam and Eve showed their love for God by walking and talking with him and by obeying him. Caring for his world was both their task and their joy.

But then something happened. Adam and Eve disobeyed and broke trust with God. Their evening strolls with him ended, and their joy washed away in a wave of guilt. Adam and Eve's sin passed to all humankind. Their son Cain murdered his brother Abel. Humans eventually became so wicked and corrupt that God regretted even creating them. God wiped out all of them except Noah and his family with a terrible flood.

But the flood couldn't wash away sin. Sin increased again until people got together to build a city with a high tower to make a name for themselves. They wanted to be independent from God. God foiled their plan by confusing their common language. But what could he do to turn around people's wicked nature?

The Tower of Babel by Gustave Doré, 1833–1883.

God's Plan

God did not let evil have the last word. He had a plan to bridge the canyon between himself and humankind. God would show people how to live righteously before him. He started with one person, Abraham, and built a God-fearing nation from him. That nation could show the rest of the world what God expected. It took many years for the story to reach its high point. Hundreds of Old Testament stories took place before Jesus, the

Messiah, came and defeated sin and death. We're going to review a big chunk of those stories this year.

Your story is one of the millions of stories that will be told until Jesus comes again. The beginning of a new year is a good time for you to review not only some of the stories from last year but also your own story.

2 — — ➤ The Birth of God's People

Bible Reference: Genesis 12, 15, 17

Have you ever felt like saying, "Please be patient with me; I'm not sure about anything anymore, and I don't know where I'm going or what I'm supposed to do!" If you are like most people, you have probably felt this way at least once or twice. Sometimes the expectations of parents and teachers are overwhelming, especially when you don't know exactly what they want. You might want to shout, "I don't get it!"

Do you suppose that Abram might have said to God, "I don't get it. I'm not sure I understand exactly what you want"? After all, he was a nomad, like the other people living in that part of the Middle East. He herded flocks from place to place, looking for water and green pastures. Then one day God came to Abram and told him about an incredible plan to heal the relationship between God and humans. God said, "I'm going to make a great nation out of you, Abram. And, by the way, you will be a blessing to all the people of the world!" Do you suppose that Abram understood God's promises and expectations very well?

A shepherd tends his sheep and goats on the hills near Jericho.

He didn't, and it's no wonder. He and his wife, Sarai, didn't even have a son, and they were getting old. In this lesson you will find out how Abram lacked understanding. But what's amazing is that God did not get angry with Abram. He patiently revealed himself and more of his plan to Abram and Sarai. God gave them time to absorb the astounding information, and then he told them what he expected from his people. He changed their names to Abraham and Sarah, and then he gave them a physical sign so they wouldn't forget. Do you know the New Testament sign of God's covenant with Abraham?

Abram/Abraham

> **Who was he and where was he from?** Abram was the son of Terah. He was born in about 1900 B.C. in Ur, a prosperous city on the banks of the Euphrates River in southern Mesopotamia. Ur was in the southern section of Mesopotamia called Sumer (home of the Sumerians, inventors of an advanced system of writing). Ur was the center of Mesopotamia's pagan culture.

The Departure of Abraham by Josef Molnar, 1850.

> **Where did his travels take him and his family?** After Abram married his half-sister Sarai, they moved to Haran in northern Mesopotamia. They lived there until Abram was 75, when God told Abram to migrate to Canaan. When Abram's family reached Canaan, they wandered from place to place to find water and food for their flocks; they lived outside cities and didn't associate much with the Canaanites. During a long drought the family traveled to Egypt, returning when the drought ended.

> **What was so special about him?** Abram is remembered as a great man of faith, a friend of God, and the man through whom God's Old Testament covenant with his people came. God changed Abram's name to Abraham when he made the covenant with him.

In the last lesson you reflected on your own spiritual journey. In this lesson you will look at the beginning of humankind's spiritual journey back to God. The God who patiently revealed himself to Abraham is just as patient with us.

3 ‑ ‑ ➤ The Birth of God's Nation

Bible Reference: Genesis 27–50; Exodus 12;
Deuteronomy 6, 28; Joshua 2–4, 24

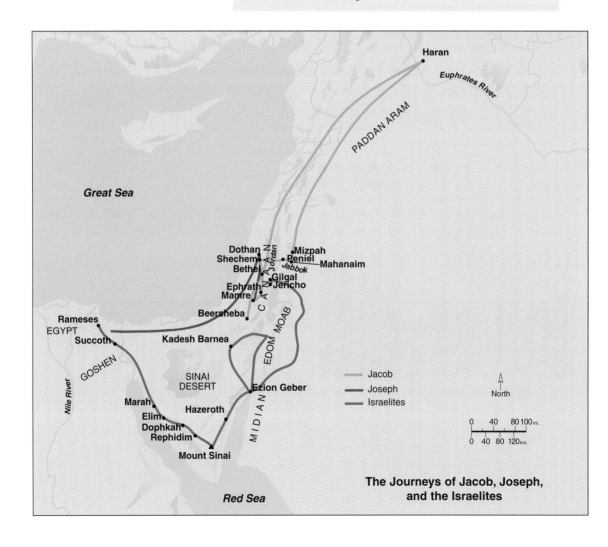

The Journeys of Jacob, Joseph,
and the Israelites

4 – – – – ➤ The Beginning of the Kingdom of Israel

**Bible Reference: 1 Samuel 13:3–14; 15:1–22;
2 Samuel 7:18–28; 12:9–17, 24–25**

The story of Joshua is filled with battles against the Canaanites. Joshua knew how attractive and how deadly Canaanite religious practices were. He knew that the Israelites' covenant relationship with God would shatter if the Israelites joined in these pagan practices. Near the end of his life at Shechem Joshua asked the people to choose whom they would serve, and they said, "We too will serve the Lord because he is our God."

Joshua died, and eventually so did the whole generation of Israelites who had entered Canaan with him. Before long God's promises were forgotten and the new generation began to serve the Canaanite gods. They didn't seem to care about the requirements of God's covenant with them. And so began a terrible cycle. The people worshiped the gods of the surrounding people; God punished them by sending raiders who plundered them and carried many off into slavery; the people cried to God for deliverance; God sent judges to save them. As long as a judge was alive, the people followed God. When the judge died, the people became more corrupt than before.

Canaanite god.

This cycle repeated itself over and over. But as time continued the judges became less and less worthy to lead God's people, and the people became less and less interested in repenting. God's attempt to raise a nation to be a light to the other nations seemed to be a miserable failure. But God didn't give up on his people. God gave his people one more judge: Samuel.

Samuel was a good and faithful judge, but his sons were dishonest and corrupt. They accepted bribes from the rich and treated the poor unjustly. Their reputation made the people wish for a change in leadership. They did not want to be under the thumb of these two men. They were also attracted to the leadership styles of the people around them. They wanted a king who would lead them in battle. So they asked Samuel to choose a king to lead them.

Samuel was worried about their desire for a king, but God instructed him to anoint Saul as God's nagid. Do you remember the difference between a pagan king and a nagid?

Nagids and Meleks

When someone mentions the word *king*, do you think of someone wearing a dazzling crown sitting on a golden throne, or perhaps a mighty warrior leading his troops into battle? That's the kind of king the Israelites wanted. The kings of the pagan nations around Israel were *meleks*, military leaders with absolute power. Israel wanted to "be like all the other nations, with a king to lead us and to go out before us and fight our battles" (1 Samuel 8:20).

But God knew that it would not be good for the Israelites to have a king like that. So he gave them a *nagid*, a ruler chosen and anointed by God to be responsible for the nation's faithfulness to the covenant.

King Tutankhamen's golden throne.

Unit 2
The Kingdom Is Divided

1 ▬ ▬ ▬ ▬ ➜ Israel's Golden Age

Bible Reference: 1 Kings 10—11:25;
Deuteronomy 17:14–20

In Shining Splendor

Solomon was one of those golden people who seemed to have it all. He had it as good as the fisherman's wife in the old folktale—maybe even better. He was king over a powerful, rich nation chosen by God. He was at peace with the neighboring nations. He had built palaces, walls, terraces, ships, and God's temple. He lived lavishly, stockpiling gold, silver, spices, and jewels. In addition, Solomon had God-given wisdom, and he knew that God's people were to be a source of hope and light to the Gentiles.

Under the Glitter

In some ways Solomon was a great ruler. According to 1 Kings 10, Solomon was doing very well indeed. But what makes a king truly great? What are the qualities of an ideal king? Early in the history of Israel, God gave some guidelines for genuine leadership. These are recorded in Deuteronomy 17:14–20. Did Solomon have all of the qualifications?

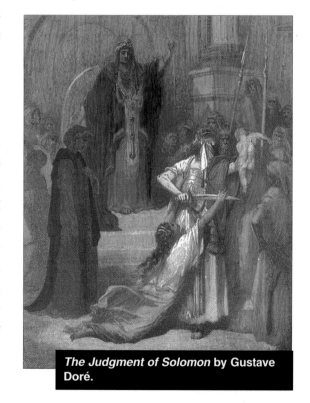

The Judgment of Solomon by Gustave Doré.

What's a Covenant?

A covenant is a contract between two parties. God was the powerful partner in Old Testament covenants, and his people pledged him loyalty and obedience. God laid down his requirements at Mount Sinai when he gave his laws to Moses. These laws are recorded in the first five books of the Old Testament. If the people obeyed God, he would bless them. But if they broke the covenant, God's people would suffer terrible disasters.

Solomon's Problems

Solomon's reign had been peaceful. In fact, it marked the high point of the kingdom of Israel. The queen of Sheba's visit showed that Israel could be a light to the Gentiles. Unfortunately, Solomon didn't always follow his own advice, and his failures tore the kingdom apart.

2 ➡ Jeroboam, the Revolutionary

Bible Reference: 1 Kings 11:26–40;
1 Kings 12:25—13:6

A sensitive student once said that teachers were often fooled by words that seemed so sincere inside the classroom. In her opinion, students often used pious language in order to look good in the eyes of the teacher, but the students' talk didn't have much to do with the way they acted in the hallway.

Scheming to be "top dog" is nothing new. In this lesson we are going to see a king who had the chance of a lifetime. He needed only to trust God's promises and obey God's law.

Jeroboam's Self-Defeating Strategy

Jeroboam was a clever man and a successful administrator for Solomon. Then a prophet of God promised him the kingdom. Jeroboam found it difficult to trust God to carry out his promise. Perhaps Jeroboam thought that God couldn't handle it on his own.

Jeroboam took the situation into his own hands. He knew that faithful worship creates loyalty and unity, and he did not want the people of his kingdom to have divided loyalties. So Jeroboam changed the religious practices of the people of the northern kingdom. He drew their religious loyalty away from Jerusalem.

To do this, Jeroboam created new worship centers and new practices that imitated faithful worship. He wanted the calves to represent God's presence but exhibit a little more pizzazz. Jeroboam's calves looked a little like the Canaanite god Baal perched on a bull's back. But God's presence was supposed to be represented only by the ark in the temple. The ark contained the tablets of the law of the covenant, and worship was never to be separated from God's law.

Jeroboam broke God's covenant and led the people to disobey God's commandments. He found not only terrible and immediate consequences but also amazing, immediate mercy.

The ark of the covenant chiseled on a stone from Capernaum.

3 ▬ ➤ Jeroboam, Are You Listening?

Bible Reference: 1 Kings 13–14

Do you remember when you first learned to read? Much of the time during your first years in school was devoted to reading. As science entered your world, you learned to read God's creation. You learned how to read time and seasons. You learned about rocks and trees. Another kind of reading is "reading" people. Reading people means paying close attention to what they say and do in order to know what kind of people they are. Sometimes appearances are deceiving. In the last lesson we saw that Jeroboam tried to make the people believe that he was a genuine, God-fearing Israelite. In fact, his motives were mixed, and his religion got mixed up with Canaanite practices.

Two Prophets and a Lion

In this lesson we're going to take another look at Jeroboam through two stories and three prophets. In the first story the man of God from Judah

The Prophet Slain by a Lion by Gustave Doré.

meets a deceptive prophet from Israel. God reveals himself to Jeroboam, to the people, and to us. This story is found in 1 Kings 13:7–34.

A Boy and a Prophet

In the second story we find Jeroboam back to his old tricks. Even though his son's illness shook him up and he wanted to know what would happen, he tried to trick the prophet and manipulate the message. This story is found in 1 Kings 14:1–18.

Sometimes we try to trick ourselves and others by hiding our real intentions from others and perhaps from ourselves. But God never tries to trick us. God called to Jeroboam to try to keep him on track. Was Jeroboam listening? If we listen and watch closely we can see that our heavenly Father was merciful to Jeroboam by letting Abijah die a natural death and be buried.

Sometimes a personal crisis shakes us up and makes us seek out God. This happened to Jeroboam when his son Abijah became ill. Jeroboam sent his wife in disguise to Ahijah to find out what would happen to the boy.

The Prophets' Job

God chose the prophets to speak for him to the kings and the people. That was their main job. Prophets also foretold the future. Their predictions applied to the immediate future and were usually fulfilled within a short time, although many prophecies also had a long-term fulfillment.

Amos by Gustave Doré.

During the early period of the divided kingdom, many of the prophets (such as Elijah and Elisha) lived in communities or schools. These prophets often performed miracles to demonstrate God's power. Although they spoke the word of the Lord, they did not leave a written record of their messages. Later prophets (such as Isaiah and Jeremiah) did not live in communities. They left poetic, written records of the words God had sent them to speak. Miracles did not play as great a role in the later prophets' ministry.

Whether they were preaching prophets or writing prophets, their messages all included three themes. One theme was faithful worship. A second theme was that judgment would come to the people who disobeyed the covenant's requirements. A third theme was hope. The prophets spoke words of encouragement on God's behalf. They continually reminded the kings and the people of the blessings that awaited God's obedient children.

Deuteronomy 18:14–22 outlines the distinction between a true prophet and a false prophet. True prophets spoke the words of God himself. False prophets spoke only what was pleasing in order to gain status or income in the king's court.

4 ━ ━ ━ ━ ━ ➤ A Look Around

Israel's Neighborhood

Imagine living in a neighborhood where you can't trust your neighbors. You're sure that they are just waiting to take what you own. That would affect how you get along with them, wouldn't it?

That's a bit like the situation God's people faced during the years of the divided kingdom. Israel had a strategic position. Because of its central location and access to the sea, trade routes had crossed the area for centuries. The deserts to the south and east made travel through Israel even more

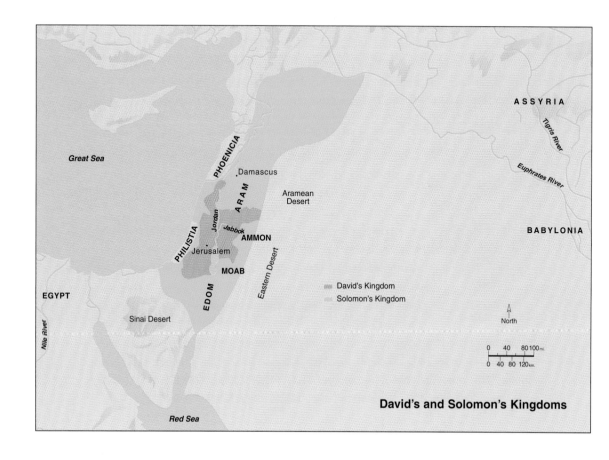

David's and Solomon's Kingdoms

attractive. Israel's neighbors envied its prime location. They constantly watched and waited for signs of weakness so that they could move in.

Let's take a brief look at Israel's neighbors. Becoming familiar with their names and locations will help you better understand the Bible stories we'll be studying.

Egypt

Egypt had been a great world power for centuries, but its power was declining by the time David became king. Although Egypt was not a threat to a united Israel under Solomon, Shishak, Egypt's pharaoh, saw his opportunity when Israel split into two kingdoms. He invaded Jerusalem and carried off the temple treasures. Just like that, Solomon's wealth and pride were gone.

Shishak was so proud of his success against Israel that he wrote an account of it on a temple wall. That account can still be read today. Shishak wrote that he plundered cities in both the southern and northern kingdoms.

When the Assyrians flexed their muscles about 150 years later, they mocked Egypt's weakness. Isaiah 36:4–6 tells

This wall at Karnak, similar to Shishak's wall, has a list of defeated enemies on the left side.

how the king of Assyria described Egypt as "that splintered reed." He compared Egypt to a sliver!

Edom

Edom was located to the southeast of Judah. The Edomites were distant relatives of the Israelites because they were the descendants of Esau, Jacob's brother. But there was little love between these relatives. Remember how the Edomites refused to let the Israelites pass through their country on their way into the Promised Land?

The Book of Samuel tells us that David won the Edomites' undying hatred. He defeated them in battle and made them subject to Israel. Edom's hatred for God's people continued throughout Israel's history. When the Babylonians finally captured Jerusalem, the Edomites urged them to destroy the city. Edom was not large and powerful, but it was a bitter enemy of Israel—an enemy to be watched.

Philistia

Along the coast of the Mediterranean Sea, between Israel and Egypt, was the land of the Philistines. The Philistines were a constant problem for Israel. During the period of the judges, God allowed the Philistines to oppress the Israelites when they worshiped idols. The threat of the Philistines was probably what led to Israel's request for a king.

Because the Philistines controlled the iron industry, their army had metal weapons and chariots. That made their army stronger than the Israelite army. With God's help, David finally drove the Philistines out of Israel and even attacked Philistia.

Moab

Moab was just east of the Dead Sea. The Moabites were related to the

This picture of Moab was taken from the west side of the Dead Sea.

Israelites through Lot, Abraham's nephew. Like the Edomites, they had refused to allow the Israelites to pass through their land as they approached the Promised Land. One Moabite king, Balak, even hired Balaam to curse the Israelites, but God caused Balaam to bless the Israelites instead. The Book of

Ruth suggests that later there was free travel and a friendly relationship between Moab and Israel.

Moab was another nation that David defeated in battle. The Moabites were forced to pay tribute (taxes) to Israel. To keep the peace with Moab, Solomon took Moabite wives and worshiped their god Chemosh. Moab gained independence from Israel after Solomon's death.

Ammon

The Ammonites were a cruel, fierce people who lived north of Moab and east of the Jordan River. They, like the Moabites, were descendants of Lot. God told the Israelites to avoid battle with them. David later defeated Ammon and even took the gold crown of Ammon's king.

Ammon influenced Israel in another way. During Solomon's rule, the Ammonite worship of Molech crept into Israel.

Phoenicia (Sidon)

Phoenicia was a small country on the coast of the Mediterranean Sea. The Phoenicians were excellent sailors and sea traders. Of all the nations surrounding Israel, Phoenicia was the most neighborly.

Solomon made a famous deal with the Phoenician King Hiram. Hiram supplied equipment, skilled labor, and lumber to build the temple. In return, Solomon provided food for Hiram's royal household. Later Solomon owed Hiram so much that he temporarily handed over 20 of Israel's towns to Hiram as a pledge that the debt would be repaid.

When Aram threatened both nations, Israel and Phoenicia made a treaty. To seal it, Israel's King Ahab married a Phoenician princess named Jezebel. A royal marriage was a common way to seal a deal. But this deal was not a good one for Israel because Jezebel was a dedicated worshiper of Baal.

Aram

Aram was located just northeast of Israel, but its borders were never clear because its territory was divided into several small kingdoms. Each kingdom had a main city with its own king. The most powerful city-kingdom was Damascus, which later became the capital city of all of Aram. Aram was rich in farmland, and it was larger and more powerful than Israel.

David controlled the Arameans during his reign. After Solomon's death, Aram wanted to expand to the south. When Asa (the third king of Judah) asked the Arameans for help against Baasha (the third king of Israel), he opened the way for many Aramean invasions.

The Arameans were a dangerous enemy of the Israelites. The only time these two nations formed a treaty was when they banded together against a more powerful force, the Assyrians.

Assyria

Assyria was located northeast of Aram, between the Tigris and Euphrates Rivers. During Israel's early years in the Promised Land, Assyria was not a threat. About 100 years after Solomon's death, the Assyrians began to gain strength and expand. They became a dreaded enemy. Their army was a war machine that flattened everything in its path. Their cruel soldiers skinned captives alive or cut off their heads and stacked them in piles.

Many prophets warned the kings of Israel and Judah that if they were not faithful to God the Assyrians would surely conquer them. And that's exactly what happened. From about 750 to 722 B.C. Assyria launched a series of invasions against the northern kingdom of Israel. The final blow came when the Assyrians captured the capital city, Samaria, in 722 B.C. The Assyrians followed their usual method to make sure Israel wouldn't organize a new rebellion: they shipped many Israelites to other lands and replaced them with a mixture of foreign people.

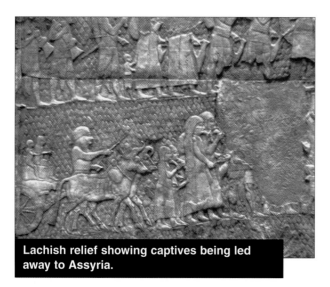

Lachish relief showing captives being led away to Assyria.

Summary

Before Israel became a nation, Egypt was the greatest power in the Near East. Israel was the greatest power under David and Solomon (1010 B.C. to 930 B.C.). During this time Israel's neighbors were forced to pay tribute; none of them was strong enough to consider making any moves against Israel.

But when a nation is divided, it cannot last for long. When the tribes split into two kingdoms, Israel's neighbors began to look for opportunities to escape Israel's rule. Some wanted revenge.

Assyria grew stronger and stronger and became the most feared of all nations in the Near East. The Assyrian empire swallowed the northern kingdom of Israel in 722 B.C. But the Assyrian empire didn't last long. By the time Judah was captured (606–586 B.C.), the Babylonians had defeated the Assyrians.

God's people were supposed to bless their neighbors. God had called them to be a light in the world. Israel was in an ideal central spot to do that. But how could God's people be a light when their nation was split in two? Even worse, they began to fight each other.

5 ▬ ▬ ➤ Something Rotten in Israel

Bible Reference: 1 Kings 15:25–16:28

Appearances Can Be Deceiving

Have you ever had to choose between a shiny, red apple and a small, pale one? Perhaps you chose the shiny, red one, took a bite, and found that its grainy, mushy texture made you wish you had chosen the small, pale one. Some people can fool you like that. They look marvelous, their reputation is great, and they even go to church regularly. But it's what's on the inside that counts.

In this lesson we are going to look at one of the "red apples" of the kingdom of Israel. His name was King Omri. Anyone looking at his reputation and achievements would certainly say that he was a great king. Something was wrong at the core, though. He and the four kings preceding him all had soft, mushy centers. Their loyalty was not directed to worshiping and serving the true God, but toward themselves—their own interests, achievements, and goals. Does that sound rotten to you?

Faithful or Not?

That's what the writer of the Book of Kings asked himself about these five kings of Israel. He didn't ask whether they were popular or successful. He only asked, "Were they faithful to God?"

The writer of the Book of Kings wrote for one purpose: to tell the people

The Chain of Events in 1 Kings 15:25—16:28.

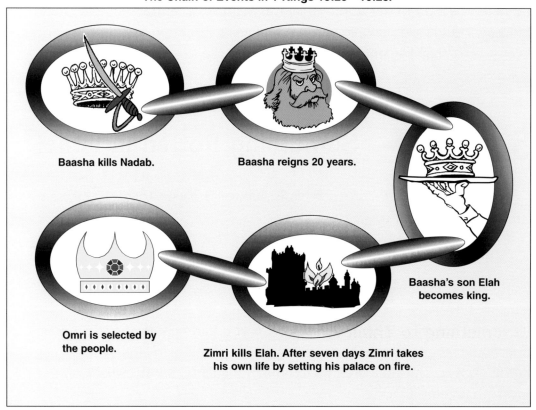

Baasha kills Nadab.

Baasha reigns 20 years.

Baasha's son Elah becomes king.

Zimri kills Elah. After seven days Zimri takes his own life by setting his palace on fire.

Omri is selected by the people.

Did you know that 1 and 2 Kings are actually one work, called in Hebrew tradition simply "Kings"? The people who made the Greek translation of the Old Testament divided it into two books.

So, who wrote Kings? There's not much evidence about who really wrote it, but whoever wrote it was familiar with the Book of Deuteronomy.

You can probably guess what's in the Book of Kings—lots of information about kings. It's a history of the kings of Israel and Judah in the light of God's covenants. One of the book's themes is that the kings' welfare depended on how well they carried out their covenant responsibilities.

1 Kings covers about 120 years of Israel's history. A lot happened during that time:

- David died and Solomon became king (1 Kings 1–2).
- Solomon built the temple that was to become the focus of worship for the Jews (1 Kings 3–11).
- The kingdom split into a northern kingdom (Israel) and a southern kingdom (Judah) after Solomon's death (1 Kings 12).
- The rest of 1 Kings tells the stories of the different kings of Israel and Judah. Israel had a very shaky monarchy, a constant cycle of a king being killed or overthrown only to be replaced by another king, who was then killed or overthrown. Things were more stable in Judah because the kingship was handed down from generation to generation to David's descendants.

Oh, don't forget that God was still working through the prophets Elijah and Elisha. You can read about them in the Book of Kings too.

in exile about God's dealings with his people and their response to God and his covenant law. The writer selected events and stories to fit his purpose. He cut to the core of the matter in the lives of all five of these kings. If the kings and the nation kept the covenant, God would bless them; if they broke the covenant, they would have problems.

Something to Think About

- What choices made the kings succeed or fail?
- What things determine success or failure today?

6 ━ ━ ➡ A Prophet, Some Ravens, a Widow, and Her Son

Bible Reference: 1 Kings 17;
Deuteronomy 30:14–16

Has a neighbor or an aunt or an uncle ever told you that you are just like your brother or sister? How does it make you feel? Is it a compliment, or does it make you cringe? Most of us do not like to be molded into our family's pattern. Even in Moses' time, the young people of Israel knew that they had to choose a pattern for their future. Read Deuteronomy 30:14–16.

The Background

There was a definite pattern in Ahab's family. Do you remember what Ahab's father, Omri, was like? Ahab did not have to follow Omri's example. He could have chosen life, but he chose the way of death instead. Under the rule of Ahab and Jezebel, the Israelites did not look to God, the true

Elijah Fed by the Ravens by James J. Tissot, 1836–1902.

source of fertility and rain and life. Instead, they worshiped Baal—a fertility god, a man-made creation.

As you think about this story, remember the widow and her choice to follow God and the way of life even though her family and friends worshiped Baal. Remember that just as God sent Elijah to encourage the widow, he will certainly walk with you so that you can choose life!

All Purpose Olive Oil

Imagine that you live in a small village in Palestine today. Because your family is poor, you rely on ancient methods to process your olive crop. One of your tasks is to help stomp the oil out of the olives. Yes, you will actually wash your feet (we hope) and then climb into a tub and stomp on the olives until they are broken into a pulp. Then you will gently pour the oily olive pulp into a fine mesh basket to strain it. Finally, you'll fill clean pottery jars with the precious oil.

Why is this oil so precious? Your family might make a nice profit if the oil buyer decides to buy your olive oil. He buys only the best oil as he travels from village to village. Your olive oil might even end up at a fancy New York restaurant where health-conscious Americans use olive oil instead of butter.

In Bible times the people of Israel used olive oil not only for cooking but also for anointing—like we use body lotion. They also used it to keep wounds soft so that they would heal better. Olive oil was also used as a fuel for lamps. If you had lived then, one of your weekly tasks might have been to fill the household lamps with olive oil. Olive oil burned brightly and was the only oil available for fuel.

Olive trees are amazing. Some actually bear fruit for hundreds of years. Experts think that some modern olive trees are over a thousand years old. Sometimes new trees shoot up from an old stump, but more often a good olive branch is grafted to a wild olive tree.

7 ━━➤ The Contest at Mount Carmel

Bible Reference: 1 Kings 18

The following reading tells the story of the showdown between God and Baal.

Narrator 1: The long drought had brought famine to the land of Israel. King Ahab had been looking high and low for Elijah. Meanwhile, Queen Jezebel had been hunting down and killing prophets of the Lord. Finally, after three years, God sent Elijah to Ahab.

Ahab: Is that you, you troubler of Israel?

Elijah: I have not made trouble for Israel. But you and your father's family have. You have abandoned the Lord and his commands and followed Baal. Call all the people of Israel to meet me on Mount Carmel. Bring along the 450 priests of Baal who eat at Jezebel's table.

Narrator 2: So Ahab did exactly as Elijah commanded. When they all were assembled on Mount Carmel, Elijah greeted them with a challenge.

Elijah: How long will you waver between two opinions? If the Lord is God, follow him! If Baal is God, follow him!

Narrator 3: The people had been trying to worship both God and Baal. But they said nothing to Elijah's challenge. Then Elijah said:

Elijah: I am the only prophet of the Lord left, but there are 450 prophets of Baal here. Get two bulls for us to sacrifice. Let them choose the one they want and cut it into pieces and put it on the wood for sacrifice, but do not set fire to it. I will do the same with the other bull. Then let the prophets call on their god, and I will call on the name of the Lord. The god who answers with fire—he is God.

The people: What you say is good.

Narrator 4: So the prophets of Baal chose their bull and put it on the altar. Then they began to pray to Baal.

Prophets of Baal: O Baal, answer us! Hear us, O Baal!

Narrator 5: They prayed like this all morning long, but there was no response. No one answered. Then they danced around the altar. Around and around they went, shouting to Baal.

Prophets of Baal: Hear us, O Baal. Send down fire, O Baal! Hear us, O Baal. Answer us, Baal!

Narrator 1: At noon Elijah began to mock them.

Elijah (in a sarcastic voice): Shout louder! Maybe Baal is sleeping in today! Maybe he's on vacation! Surely if he is a god, he will hear you!

Narrator 2: When they heard this, the prophets of Baal began to shout even louder and began to slash themselves with knives and swords.

Prophets of Baal: Hear us, O Baal. Hear and answer us, Baal! Send your fire, mighty Baal! See our blood and our sacrifice! Hear us, O Baal. Hear and answer us, Baal!

Narrator 3: This wild behavior continued until evening, but nothing happened. No one answered them. Then Elijah stepped forward.

Phoenician Baal.

Elijah (to the people): Come here to me.

Narrator 4: Then Elijah took 12 stones, one for each of Jacob's tribes. As he used the 12 stones to make an altar in the name of the Lord, he said,

Elijah: Your name shall be Israel. You are God's covenant people.

Narrator 5: Then he dug a trench around the altar. The people wondered what he was up to. He arranged the wood on the altar, cut the bull, and laid pieces on the wood. Then he turned to some men nearby and said,

Elijah: Fill four large jars with water, and pour it on the offering and on the wood.

Narrator 1: When they had finished, Elijah said,

Elijah: Do it again.

Narrator 2: They did it again.

Elijah: Do it a third time.

Narrator 3: They did it a third time. The water drenched the offering, the wood, and even filled the trench. Then Elijah prayed.

Elijah: O Lord, God of Abraham, Isaac, and Israel, let it be known today that you are God in Israel and that I am your servant and have done these things today at your command. Answer me, O Lord, so these people will know that you, O Lord, are God, and that you are turning their hearts back again.

Narrator 4: Suddenly fire fell from heaven and burned up the sacrifice, the wood, the stones, the water in the trench, and even the dampened soil! When the people saw this, they fell flat on their faces in fear and awe.

The people: The Lord—he is God! The Lord—he is God!

Elijah: Seize the prophets of Baal. Don't let anyone get away!

Narrator 5: The people seized all the prophets of Baal, and Elijah killed them. Then Elijah climbed to the top of Mount Carmel. He bent low to the ground, put his face between his knees, and humbled himself before God. He said to his servant,

Elijah: Go and look toward the sea.

Servant: There is nothing there. The sky is clear.

Elijah: Go back and look again.

Narrator 1: This happened seven times. After the seventh time, Elijah's servant had something to report.

Servant: A cloud as small as a man's hand is rising from the sea.

Elijah: Go and tell Ahab, "Hitch up your chariot and hurry back to your palace before the rain stops you."

Narrator 2: The sky grew dark, the wind began to blow, and then a heavy rain fell. Ahab rode off in his chariot.

Narrator 3: With his cloak tucked in his belt and God's power sustaining him, Elijah ran ahead of Ahab's chariot.

Narrator 4: And the thunder and lightening of the Lord pursued Ahab all the way to Jezreel.

8 — — — ➤ The Mountain of God

Bible Reference: 1 Kings 19

Stopped in His Tracks

An Olympic diver recently told about being stopped in his tracks, or, to be exact, in his swimming pool. He had won several medals at the Olympic games four years earlier and felt like he was on top of the world. He was talented, good-looking, and glib. He was as comfortable talking on network television as he was talking with his brother. After the games ended, he made lots of money by simply endorsing a swimsuit maker. He even made guest appearances on late-night television. But the high didn't last, and he became depressed. All of his hopes, his plans, and his energy drained into a dark pit of despair, and he wanted his life to end. His self-pity seemed boundless.

On the Run

After the victory on Mount Carmel, Elijah should have been rejoicing in God's triumph, but he wasn't singing praises. Some say that he was depressed; others say that he was so preoccupied with his own point of view that he lost sight of God. What brought Elijah to this low point?

First of all, Elijah must have been bone tired. He had just finished a long journey—he had run for his life from Jezebel, traveling first from Jezreel to Beersheba (about 100 miles) and then continuing for another day into the desert. Elijah was probably also tired of battling with Israel, trying to get the people to change their evil ways. Perhaps he felt that all his work had been for nothing. Although Elijah knew that God was all-powerful, he was convinced that Jezebel's hit men were going to kill him.

Elijah had forgotten God's faithfulness. He was ready to give up on Israel. He saw no future for God's people.

God's Cure

Instead of using a display of great power, God came to Elijah with a "gentle whisper." The gentle whisper shows God's patience, compassion, and grace for Elijah and for Israel. What a contrast to the wind, fire, and earthquake—images of judgment and wrath! Elijah's preaching had been full of judgment. He needed to learn compassion for God's people.

God's appearance to Elijah renewed the prophet's hope and energy. Elijah learned that the Lord is not limited to an earthquake, wind, or fire. God's power is also not limited to Israel. God could work in Aram as well as in Israel. God is the King of all creation.

When God told Elijah to anoint three people, he showed Elijah that his work would continue. Elijah was not alone.

By the way, the diver recovered and went on to compete again. So did Elijah.

Life under the Broom Tree

The Bible tells us that Elijah sat under a broom tree. Have you ever heard about broom trees?

The broom tree is a large shrub that burns very well. Even if a broom tree fire is put out, the inside of the wood continues to burn. People who have covered broom tree fires with sand have found the embers still hot after several months! To keep warm at night, desert people would find a

broom tree, light a fire, and when the coals were hot, bury them several inches deep in the sand. Then the traveler could lie down on the sand for a warm sleep. Maybe that's what Elijah did. Perhaps the angel used the coals to bake the bread.

9 ‒ ‒ ‒ ‒ ▶ A Typical Pagan King

Bible Reference: 1 Kings 21

God's Kingdom

In the kingdom of God life is good and just. People care about each other. Leaders in the kingdom of God—whether they are kings, prophets, priests, or parents—must protect this kind of life. These leaders rule by serving people, by doing what's best for them. They know their authority comes from God. They rule under God and for God.

Ahab, the King of Cowards

But Ahab didn't rule in that way. For one thing, he was totally influenced by his wife. Jezebel, the pagan princess, acted with incredible self-assurance, mostly because she did not place herself in God's covenant family. Jezebel believed that because she was queen and Ahab was king, they could take whatever they wanted whenever they wanted it.

Jezebel rejected God's law concerning land. At Mount Sinai God had given the land to the people in sacred trust. Ahab didn't even have Jezebel's flimsy excuse of a pagan childhood. Ahab knew what God required of him, but he didn't take

Omri, Ahab, Jeroboam II, and many other Israelite kings lived in this palace.

charge of the situation. Ahab looked the other way when crafty Jezebel framed Naboth and had him stoned. And when all the dirty work was done, Ahab took over Naboth's land. What a leader!

Of course God did not ignore Ahab's crime against Naboth. Elijah confronted Ahab and pronounced a curse on him. He used the gruesome curse found in Deuteronomy 28:16—"You will be cursed in the city and cursed in the country." Elijah told Ahab that "dogs will eat those belonging to Ahab who die in the city, and the birds of the air will feed on those who die in the country" (1 Kings 21:24).

10 — — — ➔ Will the Real Prophet Please Stand Up?

> **Bible Reference: 1 Kings 22**

Cast Narrator
Ahab, king of Israel
False prophets
Micaiah, a prophet of God

Jehoshaphat, king of Judah
Messenger
Zedekiah, a false prophet

Scene One

Narrator: King Jehoshaphat of Judah is paying a social visit to King Ahab of Israel. Dressed in their royal robes, the two kings are sitting on their thrones near the gate of Samaria, Israel's capital city.

Jehoshaphat: Ahab, I've been here for three days, and you still haven't told me what's wrong. Come out with it! I know *something* is bothering you.

Ahab: All right, I'll tell you. It's just that—it's just that I can't get Syria off my mind.

Jehoshaphat (showing surprise): Syria? Why Syria? They haven't bothered you since you defeated them three years ago. C'mon, Ahab, stop worrying. Enjoy this time of peace.

Ahab (loudly, angrily): Stop worrying? I can't forget that Syria still holds Ramoth Gilead! That city belongs to Israel. I want that city back. Do you hear me? I want it back!

Jehoshaphat (calmly): And you want me to help you get it back, right?

Ahab (smiling): Yes, that's right. Will you help me fight for Ramoth Gilead? Together we could easily win! Will your armies join mine?

Jehoshaphat: Of course. After all, our nations are like brothers. You can count on me—on my armies and my chariots, but . . . (*pauses, looks directly at Ahab, and continues quietly*) there's just one thing. We should ask the Lord first, to see if he wants us to fight Syria.

Ahab: Of course! (*impatiently calling to a messenger*) Come here at once! Go call my prophets—all 400 of them—and tell them to come to the palace immediately!

Messenger (bowing): It will be done as you say, O king.

Narrator: As the two kings wait, Ahab notices that Jehoshaphat is quiet and thoughtful. Ahab resumes his nervous pacing. Finally, the messenger returns.

Messenger (bowing): I have done as you requested, sire. All 400 prophets are here to give you God's advice.

Jehoshaphat (to himself): Why, Ahab wasn't kidding—there really are 400! But are they God's prophets or Ahab's?

Ahab: Prophets, you remember the great city of Ramoth Gilead that once belonged to Israel? Now the city is in the hands of pagans. (*Pauses, then continues loudly.*) Well, I want to get it back. Shall I go to war against Ramoth Gilead?

False prophets (in unison): Go! The Lord will deliver the city into the king's hands.

Ahab (Smiling proudly, he puts his hand on Jehoshaphat's arm.): There, you've heard it yourself. That settles it, right?

Jehoshaphat (firmly): Not so fast, Ahab. Isn't there a prophet of the Lord in your land? I'd like to ask him too.

Ahab (frowning): Well, there is someone named Micaiah, but he and I don't get along. In fact, I hate him! He never prophesies anything good about me. He always brings bad news.

Jehoshaphat: You shouldn't say that, Ahab. Please call this Micaiah.

Ahab (*grudgingly*): If you insist. Messenger, find Micaiah, and bring him here at once.

Narrator: While Jehoshaphat and Ahab wait for Micaiah, the false prophets keep urging Ahab to go to war.

Zedekiah (*displaying a pair of iron horns he has made*): See these iron horns? The Lord says you will gore the Syrians with these until they are destroyed.

False prophets: Attack! Attack! The Lord will give you the victory!

Scene Two

Narrator: The king's messenger runs to Micaiah's house and knocks on his door.

Messenger: King Ahab has sent me to bring you to him. He wants to know whether he should fight to get Ramoth Gilead back. (*He hesitates, then continues.*) You should know that all of the other prophets are predicting success for the king. For your own safety, you'd better agree with them. Speak in favor of the attack!

Micaiah: Thanks for the warning, but I can't just repeat what people want me to say. As surely as the Lord lives, I can tell the king only what the Lord tells me to say.

Scene Three

Narrator: Ahab is still pacing back and forth as Micaiah approaches. Ahab motions the prophet to enter.

Ahab: Let's get right to the point. I want to get the city of Ramoth Gilead back from the Syrians. (*He nervously rubs his hands and looks away.*) Shall I go to war, or shall I stay home?

Micaiah (*sarcastically*): Oh, by all means, attack! Attack and be victorious, for the Lord will give you the city.

Ahab (*angrily*): You're mocking me! How many times must I tell you to speak only what the Lord tells you to? Come on, hurry up and say what you really know.

Micaiah: Look me straight in the eye, Ahab. (*Ahab slowly turns to the prophet.*) I had a dream in which your army looked like scared sheep scattered across the hills without a shepherd. They didn't know what to do or where to go. Do you know why?

Ahab: Of course not! Why?

Micaiah: Because their king, Ahab, was dead!

Ahab (motioning excitedly to Jehoshaphat): Didn't I tell you that he never prophesies good things about me? Get him out of here!

Micaiah: Just a minute, I'm not finished. Do you know why you'll die? Do you know whose fault it will be?

Ahab (refusing to listen): Get him out of my sight!

Micaiah: Because you believe your prophets and Zedekiah, who tell you what you want to hear. Don't you realize that they are false prophets and liars?

Zedekiah (leaping up and slapping Micaiah in the face): You are the liar!

Ahab (stamping his foot angrily): Get Micaiah out of here. Throw him in jail! Feed him dry bread and water—just enough to keep him alive—until I return safely from the battle.

Micaiah: If you return safely, then the Lord has not spoken through me and I am a false prophet. Mark my words, all you people!

Narrator: So King Ahab of Israel and King Jehoshaphat of Judah led their armies to Ramoth Gilead. Read 1 Kings 22:29–38 to find out what happened.

Unit 3
Israel's Slide to Destruction

1 ‒ ‒ ‒ ‒ ‒ ➤ Return to the Lord

Bible Reference: Hosea 14

Not Very Popular

"That's not the way it's supposed to be!" That was Elijah's and Hosea's message, and it is God's message for us today. In this unit we will listen to God's spokesmen forcefully yet lovingly saying, "What were you thinking? God's people can't do that! Don't you understand that sinful behavior brings disaster?"

The people of Israel had turned their backs on God and their faces toward the Canaanite gods. The Israelite people were attracted to the surrounding pagan culture. They were not particularly interested in hearing from God, but the prophets insisted on telling them what God had to say. No wonder the prophets were unpopular. People didn't like what they said or the way they said it. But the prophets were really on Israel's side. They said what they did because they knew God wanted his people to change—to accept him as their God and to live for him.

You will be studying the Book of Hosea later in this unit, but for now we are going to look at God's call to repentance found in the last chapter of that book. It is the message of all the prophets: Repent! The prophets were trying to get the people to change the direction of their lives.

Repenting—Two Steps

The Bible's word for "turn around" is *repent.* Israel was walking away from the Lord, and God wanted the people to return to him. Israel had to turn away from sin and toward obedience. True repentance has two steps.

Israel first had to experience sadness and regret for walking away from God. Being sorry for sin is the first step.

The next step is to turn and actually start to walk in a new direction.

As you learn this passage, remember that Hosea urged the people to repent because he knew that God is good, full of compassion, and merciful. God has not changed. God is still full of compassion for us, and he is waiting with open arms for us to turn to him.

Read Hosea's description of repentance and the blessings that follow it in Hosea 14.

Cedars of Lebanon

Once you have smelled cedar wood, you'll never forget its pungent aroma. Long ago magnificent cedar forests covered the mountains of Lebanon, but now they are nearly gone. You will probably never see a cedar of Lebanon, but today's cedar trees are relatives of those ancient cedars.

The beautiful cedars of Lebanon were strong and graceful evergreen trees that sometimes reached a height of 100 feet. They provided shade for weary travelers, and the wood gave off a clean fresh scent when it was burned for fuel. Priests used cedar as a fuel to burn sacrifices. The fragrant resin (the stuff that oozes out of pine trees and makes your hands sticky) was used to preserve fabric and parchment. Cedar wood was also a valuable building material. Carpenters used it when they built the temple.

In Old Testament times the cedar tree symbolized God's special relationship with his people. Although you might not want to walk around smelling like a cedar chest, you might want to think about your words and actions. Do they smell sweet and clean like the cedars of Lebanon?

The Cedars Destined for the Temple by Gustave Doré.

2 ▬ ▬ ▬ ▬ ▬ ➤ Trusting in Magic

Bible Reference: 2 Kings 1–2

Trusting in Magic

When you didn't study for a test, did you ever wish that you would magically get a straight A? Many of us wish for magical changes in our lives. Wishing is much easier than working. But wanting magical solutions to problems is a little lazy and more than a little self-centered.

A belief in magic was a part of Israel's cultural setting. Many people in Israel and certainly in the surrounding countries believed that a wild, unexplainable magic governed the world. They did not know that at the dawn of time a loving, faithful God had given laws governing every aspect of

All-consuming Fire

A blazing bonfire on a crisp October evening and the flames from a fireplace in winter give off peace and comfort. But a crack of lightning may spark a forest fire that leaves a scorched expanse of terror and death.

If you return to a burned-out forest a year or two later, the new life will surprise you. Often forest fires clear out all the dead branches and choking undergrowth. The fire makes room for new plants and new growth.

In the stories of the Bible, God's presence is often announced by fire. The quiet fire of an oil lamp shows his mercy. His purifying power burns like a forest fire, sweeping out sin and making room for new life.

Watch for images of fire in the stories of the Old Testament. Watch for glimpses of fire in your own story.

existence. This loving God spoke to the people through the prophets. Prophets like Moses and Elijah revealed the biggest requirement of God's law: God wanted his people to trust him and faithfully obey his laws. If the people disobeyed God and turned away from him, he would send doom.

Because we are made in God's image, we are able to respond to God with trusting hearts. But King Ahaziah rejected God and turned to Baal-Zebub, the lord of flies, for advice about his illness.

Goodbye Elijah, Hello Elisha

Who was Elisha? Elisha was the son of Shaphat from Abel Meholah. We first read about him in 1 Kings 19:16. Elijah was told to anoint Elisha as his successor, Hazael as king over Aram, and Jehu as king of Israel. God told Elijah that Jehu would kill any who escaped the sword of Hazael, and Elisha would kill any who escaped Jehu's sword.

How was Elisha called? He was plowing with 12 yoke of oxen when Elijah found him and threw his cloak around him. Elisha killed his oxen, burned the plowing equipment to cook the meat, and gave the meat to the people to eat. Then he followed Elijah and became his attendant.

How did he take over Elijah's work? As Elijah's life neared its end, he tried to persuade Elisha to leave him. But Elisha refused. After Elijah had parted the Jordan River, he asked Elisha, "What can I do for you before I am taken from you?" Elisha asked for a double portion of Elijah's spirit—he wanted to inherit Elijah's God-given power. Elijah promised this if Elisha saw him when he was taken.

Did Elisha get that double portion? Yes. As they walked along, a chariot and horses of fire appeared and separated them; then a whirlwind carried Elijah up to heaven (2 Kings 2:11). Elisha picked up Elijah's cloak and struck the water. The water divided, and he crossed over. After that Elisha was able to speak for God and perform miracles.

Elijah's Ascent in a Chariot of Fire **by Gustave Doré.**

When Elijah confronted Ahaziah with the curse of death, Ahaziah ignored God's word. He denied the connection between his own choices and his doom. Scorning repentance, he adopted the pagan belief that he could magically eliminate this curse. He sent his soldiers to threaten Elijah. In effect he was saying, "Take it back, or I'll kill you." It was the magical, pagan way to deal with curses—try to eliminate the curse by threatening or killing the person who spoke it. It didn't work.

3 ------➤ War in Moab

> Bible Reference: 2 Kings 3; Deuteronomy
> 2:2–5, 19; Deuteronomy 20:19–20

Have you ever heard the expression, "There are two sure things in life—death and taxes"?

The people back in the days of the kings didn't get a chance to vote against their taxes. If one nation in Palestine defeated another nation, the winner usually forced the loser to pay tribute. Sometimes they demanded money, but

Silver coins found in Samaria.

sometimes they confiscated holy golden objects. (Do you remember what happened when the Egyptian king Shishak attacked Rehoboam?) Other times the winners demanded a yearly portion of the sheep and cattle herds. The losers didn't get schools, or roads, or defense for this tribute. They only got more trouble if they didn't pay up.

The relationships in Palestine were complex. The people of Israel and Judah were related to many of their neighbors. The people of Edom were descendants of Esau, and Lot's descendants included Ammon and Moab. These tribes of people were distant relatives, and their competition and hostility dated back almost to Abraham.

When the Israelites entered Canaan, the Moabites gave them all kinds of trouble and demanded tribute. Later, King David conquered the Moabites. By the time of Ahab, Israel was demanding 100,000 lambs and the wool from 100,000 sheep from Moab. Needless to say, the Moabites rebelled.

In this lesson you will see God's merciful hand in supplying the needs of the allies who went out to suppress the Moabite rebellion. You will also learn of a strange and puzzling end to the battle. What do you suppose God expected from his people after he showed such great mercy?

The Bragging Stone

Although we say it's good to be humble, listen carefully the next time your team wins a basketball game. You will probably hear about the star's awesome defensive moves more times than you care to—unless, of course, you are the star.

Mesha, king of Moab, had to wait a long time for bragging rights against Israel. Moab had been under the rule of the house of Omri, Ahab's father, for 40 years, and Mesha was sick of paying tribute to Israel.

When he finally defeated Israel around 830 B.C., Mesha carved the story on a black basalt stone. The stone really isn't very big; it is about 44 inches high, 28 inches wide, and 14 inches thick. There are only 34 lines of text. Thousands of tourists learn about Mesha's victory every year.

A German missionary and a French archaeologist discovered the stone in 1868. The archaeologist made a copy—an impression—of the text, and it was a good thing he did. The keepers of the stone realized that it was worth a great deal to the Europeans, so they broke the stone into several pieces to make more money on the deal. The impression the archaeologist made was a key to finding all the pieces of the stone and the meaning of the text. Eventually most of the stone was recovered. It is displayed at the Louvre museum in Paris today.

Which of your achievements would you carve on a bragging stone?

4 — — — — — → God Is Our Help

A Miracle Is . . .

Which of the following events do you think are miracles?
- The birth of a baby
- A beautiful sunset
- The Israelites crossing the Red Sea
- God sending a flash flood to fill the ditches
- Jesus' resurrection
- The fire and brimstone that rained on Sodom and Gomorrah
- The creation of the world
- God answering Hannah's prayer for a son
- The Egyptian magicians' throwing down their staffs and turning them into snakes

The Historical Setting for Elisha's Miracles

Women

Women in Elisha's time didn't have careers or independence. For women long ago, marriage was a life-and-death issue. After her father, a husband was a woman's only protection. If her husband died, she had no protector, no income, and little hope—unless she had a son. A son would protect her if she became a widow, and his household would shelter her when she became old. Sons also preserved the family's inheritance in the Promised Land, since women could not inherit land.

Life was hard for widows, who were usually very poor. People often looked down on them and took advantage of them. If a man died and left a debt, the people he owed money to could legally claim his widow's children as payment. Although this was supposed to be a temporary situation, the children often became permanent slaves. In spite of her desperate situation, the widow in this lesson did not turn to the popular priests of Baal. Instead, she looked to the living God and his prophet Elisha.

Firstfruits

God required his people to give him an offering of the first and the best of the harvest—the firstfruits. Sometimes the offering was honey, grapes, or bread. The part of the offering that wasn't burned was given to the priests. They didn't receive money, so they lived on the peoples' offerings. Imagine how unhappy the priests must have been when Elisha's faithful followers gave their firstfruits to the prophet.

Iron and Blacksmiths

During the time of Saul there weren't any blacksmiths in Israel. Iron weapons and tools had to come from the Philistines. You can imagine how reluctant the Philistines were to share their technology with their enemy, Israel. The Philistines hid their knowledge from the Israelites for a long time.

Some scholars think that David may have been one of the first to learn the secrets of ironworking. When he was hiding from King Saul, David spent over a year in the Philistine city of Ziklag. This would have been a good opportunity for him to learn the trade. Archaeologists have found evidence that the Israelites began to use many iron tools and weapons around 1000 B.C.

The story in today's lesson took place about 150 years after David's time. An iron axhead was still a very expensive and rare tool. That's why the prophet who lost a borrowed one was worried. He could never afford to buy another to replace it. He might have to work off the cost as a servant or slave for the owner.

Iron arrowheads and metals found in Tel Halif.

5 ▬ ▬ ▬ ▬ ▬ ▬ ➤ The Massacre

Bible Reference: 2 Kings 9–10, Hosea 1:4–5

Have you ever seen someone take revenge on a bully? We all feel a sense of satisfaction when someone bigger and stronger beats up a bully, especially if we have been victims of the bully. But what happens if the bully-beating hero gets out of control? Sometimes the cure becomes as bad as the disease. Sometimes an act of justice turns into a grab for power or popularity, and justice is forgotten.

As we have read the stories of Ahab, we've been waiting for the murderous, cruel Ahab and Jezebel to get what's coming to them. You might know Jehu best as a wild chariot driver, but in this story he becomes much more. You will probably applaud the way he enthusiastically obeys God and eliminates Baal worship from Israel. But the story takes an extremely bloody turn. As you read today's story, think about Jehu. Was he a hero?

A Burned Rock

Fire is often a sign of God's presence in Old Testament stories. God spoke to Moses in a burning bush, and the pillar of fire led the Israelites at night. What a night-light!

Jehu's men destroyed a stone sacred to Baal worshipers by burning it. Some experts believe that they heated the rock in a fire and then poured water over it. The sudden temperature change would cause the stone to shatter.

Sometimes the light of God is a comfort, and sometimes it is a purifying fire.

As this story begins, the armies of Judah and Israel are allied against the army of King Hazael of Aram at Ramoth Gilead. King Joram of Israel has retreated to recover from a wound. Jehu, one of his commanders, is sitting with fellow officers when the word of the Lord comes to him. A prophet of God anoints Jehu king of Israel, and things will never again be the same for Ahab's family.

6 ▬ ▬ ▬ ▬ ▬ ▬ ➤ Jehu's Dynasty

Bible Reference: 2 Kings 13–15:10

Have you ever heard the expression "What goes around comes around"? It wasn't easy for the people of Israel to forget the way Jehu had wiped out Baal worship. Because of his drastic measures, many government officials were dead, and the government was probably quite chaotic. The treaty with Judah was broken because Jehu had ordered the death of King Ahaziah of Judah. Jezebel's death destroyed the alliance with Phoenicia. Jehu also allowed some pagan forms of religion to flourish in Israel.

So when King Hazael of Aram attacked, there was no one to help Israel. Jehu watched the borders of his kingdom shrink. Under his son, Jehoahaz, Israel nearly lost its identity as a nation. Just a few years earlier, King Ahab had been able to launch 2,000 chariots against the Assyrians. Now

Jehoahaz had only ten chariots. The Arameans controlled the trade routes through Israel. They collected the tolls charged to caravans passing through and deprived Israel of a big source of income. Aram also demanded huge payments of tribute, which further weakened Israel's economy.

Then around the turn of the century, during Jehoahaz's reign, conditions started to improve. God had been waiting, listening for the cry of his people. Finally, Jehoahaz called on God, and God rescued Israel from Aram's power. He used the Assyrians to deliver them.

The Assyrians crushed Aram and then withdrew, because a revolt was taking place back home. (Things would have gone differently if Assyria had marched beyond Aram into Israel, but Assyria had other problems to deal with.) Jeroboam II was able to regain the territory the Arameans had taken from Jehu and Jehoahaz. Israel became almost as big and powerful as it had been during Solomon's reign.

With peace came trade and prosperity. Things had never been better. Israel's future had never looked brighter. But something was wrong.

Unfortunately, faith in God withered and died within a few years. Israel again descended into chaos. What goes around *does* come around without God's grace.

Ivory Palaces

During the time of King Jeroboam II, many people were very well off. People were optimistic and confident of God's protection.

The weaving industry flourished, and those skillful at dying fabric made a good living. Craftsmen created lovely couches for aristocrats to lounge on, and caravans from Africa brought exotic foods and other luxuries.

The king's palace in Samaria was a bigger and better version of the estates that were springing up all over Israel. Archaeologists have discovered a pool that may have provided a refreshing place for the wealthy to cool their feet. Hundreds of delicately carved ivory plaques suggest a life of beauty and luxury. Life was good for the king and for the people of the upper class.

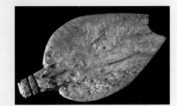

Ivory pendant.

7 ▬ ▬ ▬ ▬ ➤ The Day of the Lord

Bible Reference: The Book of Amos

Amos and the Reporters

Reporter 1: Welcome, Amos. We're glad that you have taken the time from your busy schedule to chat with us. It seems that you are making quite a stir around here.

Amos: Thank you for inviting me, but I'm not here to chat, and it's not me who's making the fuss. I didn't come here to create a name for myself. I would have been happy staying in Tekoa raising sheep and caring for fig trees.

Reporter 2: Where is Tekoa, and how is the weather there?

Amos: Tekoa is a little town in Judah south of Jerusalem, north of Hebron, and west of the Dead Sea. But Tekoa's location isn't important, and its weather isn't either.

Reporter 2: I was only trying to be polite, Amos. Relax!

Amos: Relax! You tell me to relax when all I can think about is God's message to you. Don't you want to hear it?

Reporter 1: I'll bet that our priests here in Bethel can teach you a thing or two about God. Why don't you stick around for our next worship service. We have awesome sacrifices, and the music is really inspiring.

Amos: Actually, that's what I want to talk about. God isn't interested in your fancy worship. As a matter of fact, he despises it. Have you walked through the countryside? Have you seen the hungry children and their beaten, discouraged parents? Have you ever wondered where all of your ivory couches and fine wines come from?

Reporter 1: I don't know why you're getting so excited. God promised our father David that he would always bless Israel.

Reporter 2: Our economy is booming and our neighbors are peaceful. It's a great time for Israel, so God must be blessing us.

Amos (impatiently): Don't you remember Mount Sinai? Don't you remember God's covenant laws? Have either of you read Leviticus 25?

Reporter 1: Our priests don't preach all that gloom and doom. They preach about the coming day of the Lord. You know about that, don't you, Amos?

Amos: I do. I've been writing some prophecies about the day of the Lord, and it is quite different from what you think . . .

Reporter 1 (interrupting Amos): We'd love to have you back to tell us all about it sometime, Amos, but we're out of time. We have to cover the Phoenician festival down at the Bethel shrine.

Even though most of the people in Israel had forgotten or were ignoring God's covenant requirements, God had not excused them from their responsibility to be his chosen people, his light to the nations. The laws he gave for faithful worship and healthy social conditions had not disappeared just because the people ignored them. God's law could not be broken without terrible results. Amos, the sheep herder from Tekoa, brought this stark and shocking message. Sooner or later everyone in Israel would find the time to hear and understand it.

Cows of Bashan

If you were a cow in Bashan, you lived on a fertile plain east of the Sea of Galilee. You had plenty of lush, green grass and plenty of water. Cows of Bashan were pampered in Old Testament times.

When Amos called the pampered women of Samaria "the cows of Bashan," he did not mean it as a compliment. It was an insult with a purpose. These women maintained their luxurious lives at the expense of the poor. Amos wanted them to see the sin and sickness of their lives and to repent. Unfortunately, they may have taken it as a sort of compliment, because there is no evidence that they changed their ways.

Incidentally, in Psalm 22 the bulls of Bashan symbolize the enemies of God's people. It wasn't a compliment to be called a "bull of Bashan," either.

8 ------ ➡ Not My People

Bible Reference: Hosea 1–3

The Beginning of the End

The beginning of the end came for Israel when the first King Jeroboam broke away from Judah and introduced the golden calves into Israel. That strand of disobedience polluted Israel's life from the very beginning of its existence. But at the end of the second Jeroboam's reign, Israel was sick with drunkenness, violence, and sexual perversity just as Amos had predicted.

This pagan corruption finally erupted in bloody assassinations and social chaos. In the final years of the northern kingdom, six kings ruled during a 25-year period. Four of these kings were assassinated. Assyria was on the move, taking over Israel piece by piece.

This is the setting for Hosea's ministry. He suffered through the destruction of his country and of his marriage.

A Prophet with a Hurting Heart

We see betrayal and brokenness in the world around us and in our friendships, our families, and our communities. Long ago—during violent, immoral times in Israel—there was a man named Hosea. We don't know much about him, but we do know one painful fact. He was married to a woman who was unfaithful to him, and she didn't even have the decency to be private about it. She flaunted her infidelity by becoming a prostitute and abandoning her family. The embarrassment and shame must have been unbearable. Yet God was with Hosea, even during this painful time.

Hosea didn't sink into a deep depression and drop out of life. Instead, he listened to God, who healed the marriage. God gave Hosea the insight to see his own painful story as a symbol of the broken relationship between God and his people. Hosea was able to transform his suffering into a powerful call to his fellow Israelites to repent and to return to God.

9 ▬ ▬ ▬ ➤ More Than a Fish Story

Bible Reference: Jonah 1–4

Going the Wrong Way

Have you ever been so angry that you refused to speak with your brother or sister or friend? They may have hurt your feelings, lost your new basketball, or spilled nail polish on your favorite sweatshirt. Even after they apologized, you continued to give them the silent treatment.

If you fit any part of this description, you have something in common with Jonah.

A Real Fish Story

Could the Jonah story really have happened? Bible scholars have discussed that question for many years. In 1941 a writer in a biblical journal reported that a real Jonah story had occurred somewhere near the Falkland Islands.

Jonah and the Whale from *Speculum Humane Salvationis* (15th century).

The sailors on a whaling ship had harpooned a large sperm whale, and in the confusion, one of the men was swept off the deck of the ship and feared lost. Eventually the sailors killed the whale. When they got around to cutting open its stomach, they discovered their unconscious mate still alive in there.

They revived him, and he survived. We don't know whether he ever went back to whaling, but the writer of the article reported that his exposed skin was bleached white by the whale's stomach juices.

We don't know what Jonah looked like at the end of his ordeal in the great fish, but we do know that he made a dramatic impression on the people of Nineveh.

What do you think was more important—his looks or his words?

Assyria was the bully of the Middle East. The Assyrians were known for their incredibly efficient way of fighting war and their ability to create terror. Piles of skulls and heaps of dismembered bodies generated fear and loathing in all who knew the Assyrians. The people of Israel ranked the Assyrians about as low as we rank Hitler and the Third Reich of Germany.

Now consider Jonah. God said, "Go to Nineveh and tell the people to repent. I want them to turn their hearts to me too." Jonah's response was flat-out anger. If Jonah had his way, God would get rid of the Assyrians with the same gruesome techniques that they had used on Israel. Jonah did not intend to show mercy to the Assyrians in Nineveh. But God had other intentions. Jonah became a savior in spite of himself.

10 – – – – – – ➤ Assyria Invades

Bible Reference: 2 Kings 15:8—17:6

Into the Whirlpool

Hitler's commanders may have taken a few lessons from Assyrian military history. Germany's *panzer* (armored) divisions smashed through Europe as they unleashed World War II. They used the same kind of overwhelming military force and psychological terror that the Assyrians used to conquer opposing nations. Before World War II started, Europe's leaders were unable to agree on a unified response to Hitler because they were so suspicious of each other.

Internal Problems

Chapters 15–17 of 2 Kings tell a similar unhappy story about Israel. The Bible makes it clear that Israel's unfaithfulness to God sucked Israel down to destruction.

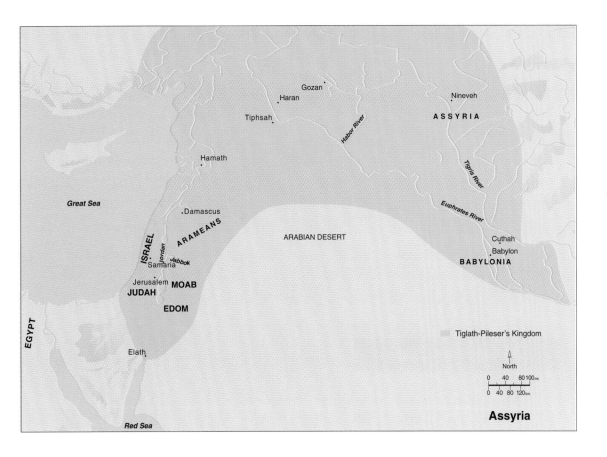

Assyria

After the death of Jeroboam II bitter suspicion, flaming immorality, and extreme idolatry erupted in Israel. Assassinations, brutality, and chaos marked the final days of the nation. One power struggle followed another for Israel's throne. The kings were afraid that their own army officers or government officials might betray or kill them.

External Threats

The Israelites were also afraid of the Assyrians. Even though Nineveh had repented, Assyria remained Israel's enemy. And the Assyrians were cruel. They were known to skin captives alive and chop off their heads. The people of Israel were used to being oppressed by Aram, but Assyria's powerful war machine was something new and shocking. Israel wasn't prepared militarily or spiritually for the coming disaster.

The last kings of Israel desperately tried to avert its doom. The first king to experience the Assyrian attacks was Menahem. Read about his response to Tiglath-Pileser in **Talents for Time**.

The next king of Israel, Pekah, decided that Israel should not be Assyria's vassal, and he ruled for a fairly long time. Possibly Pekah had support from many of the wealthy people, who were sick of paying heavy tribute to Assyria. But Pekah made a fatal mistake. When Judah refused to join his alliance with Aram, Pekah sent a force to attack Judah. The king of Judah got help from the Assyrians led by Tiglath-Pileser. In three separate invasions Tiglath-Pileser totally wiped out the Aramean-Israelite alliance.

Talents for Time

If you asked someone in ancient Israel about his talents, he would probably look at you with a very puzzled expression. He might pull out a soft pouch and carefully remove some smooth, barrel-shaped stone objects. Perhaps he would tell you that a talent was too heavy for him to carry around, but he did have some at home.

We think of a talent as a God-given ability. In Israel a talent was something quite different. A talent was a weight used for weighing silver and gold. People carried weights with them, and two people making a deal would compare their weights to keep each other honest. A shekel, which weighed one-half ounce, was used to weigh ordinary things like flour.

This stone weight has the word *pim* (⅔ of a shekel) inscribed on it in Hebrew.

When the Assyrian ruler Tiglath-Pileser (also known as Pul) threatened Israel, King Menahem tried to buy some time by giving him a huge gift—something like a bribe. He gave the Assyrian ruler 1,000 talents of silver. One talent equaled 3,000 shekels. How many pounds of silver did Menahem give to Pul?

Some experts think that at one time King Solomon's yearly income was about 666 talents of gold. So 1,000 talents was an enormous amount of silver for the people of Israel to come up with, and it bought very little time.

The End

Hoshea probably killed Pekah and took the throne of Israel because he disagreed with Pekah's foreign policy. Perhaps he thought that fighting Assyria was the fastest road to disaster. He wanted to cooperate with Assyria. In fact, Tiglath-Pileser III wrote that he put Hoshea on the throne in Israel and made Hoshea pay tribute. Hoshea was a puppet of Assyria's king.

But then Hoshea made two big mistakes: he tried to form an alliance with Egypt, and he stopped paying tribute to Assyria. His mistakes led to the final Assyrian attack and Samaria's fall. The destruction of the kingdom of Israel was complete around 721 B.C.

11 ━ ━ ━ ━ ➤ Why Did It Happen?

Bible Reference: 2 Kings 17:7–28

The End of the Story

When a wonderful story comes to an end, most people feel mildly disappointed. Something good is over. When stories about terrible events finally end, we are relieved. The stories of this unit began with King Ahaziah's hostility toward Elijah and kept going downhill. At the end Israel is bathed in blood, torn by feuding factions, and devastated by corruption. In a way it's a relief that this story is over. Yet it is sad, too. So many times a king of Israel seemed to be turning to God, and we were hopeful that their hearts would genuinely change. But that never happened.

And so we remember little glimmers of hope. We read that during Ahab's reign there were at least 7,000 people who had not bowed to Baal. We learned that some of the people of Israel went south to Judah during the time of King Hezekiah and may have returned from exile with the people of Judah. We held on to God's promise in the last verse of the Book of Amos: "I will plant Israel in their own land, never again to be uprooted from the land I have given them." A day of restoration and healing would come. God had promised it.

A Postscript

"OK," you say. "It's over for Israel. Now let's find out what happened to Judah."

But wait—there is a little more to Israel's story. After the Assyrians deported the leaders of Israel, they brought people from other parts of the Assyrian empire to live in Israel. Of course those people brought their gods with them. 2 Kings 17:25 says that lions came among the people and killed them. So, the king of Assyria sent a Jewish prophet to teach the people how to worship God properly.

Some of the poorest of the Jewish people were not deported from Israel. Together with the new immigrants they formed the people known as Samaritans. The people of Judah considered Samaritans as second-class Jews and treated them with contempt. They would not allow Samaritans to worship in Jerusalem.

The Samaritans got sick of the attitude of the people of Judah and set up a place to worship God on Mount Gerizim. By New Testament times, there was a great deal of hostility between the people of Judah and the people of Samaria. Jesus did not share the attitude of the other Jews. He told the story of The Good Samaritan, and he brought living water to the Samaritan woman. After his resurrection, Jesus told his disciples to bring the good news to the whole world— even to Samaria. Not a bad ending to a bad story!

Mount Gerizim.

Unit 4
Judah's Kings and Prophets

1 — — — ➤ Building the Background

About Chronicles

Most of the stories in this unit are taken from the Book of Chronicles. This book was probably written later than the Book of Kings, because it was written for the exiles who were allowed to return to Judah. When the rag-tag group of exiles finally returned home to Jerusalem, they found their city in shambles and their temple destroyed. They were hungry, threadbare, and discouraged.

The writer of Chronicles must have known that good stories can be powerful tools to shape people's lives. He chose stories that emphasized the family connection with Judah's hero, King David. He wanted to renew the discouraged exiles' confidence in their identity as the people of God. He wanted them to trust that God's promise to David extended to them. Their hope was symbolized by the "lamp that would never go out."

But the writer of Chronicles had a second message. Through the stories of judgment and disaster, he reminded the returned exiles of what it meant to worship God faithfully. The temple was a place of worship, a sign of faithful worship. It was the place where God revealed himself. When their grandparents had worshiped at the high places instead of the temple, the people of Judah had suffered one disaster after another. The writer didn't want the returned exiles to repeat their grandparents' mistakes.

Judah's Land and Neighbors

The land of Judah was rugged and dry. If rainfall was not plentiful and crops did not grow, people died of starvation. Death lurked close by if the

1 & 2 Chronicles

Who wrote the books of Chronicles? We don't know.

When were these books written? Probably in the fifth century B.C.

Why were they written? These books were probably written for the exiles of Judah who returned home from Babylon years later. They needed to know that they were still part of God's kingdom and that the temple and true worship were still important.

How are 1 and 2 Chronicles different from 2 Samuel and Kings? They leave out information about David's personal life and they stress Judah's history instead of Israel's. They also include a lot of information about the temple and worship.

Why did the writer include all of those boring genealogies? He wanted to show the family histories of God's people from which the messiah would come. They also prove God's faithfulness through the centuries. You can check his promises by looking at the records.

Adam — Eve
Noah
Shem Ham Japheth
Sarah — Abraham
Rebekah — Isaac
Esau Rachel — Jacob — Leah
Joseph Benjamin Reuben Simeon Levi Judah Issachar Zebulun
Boaz — Ruth
Obed
Jesse
David — Bathsheba
Solomon
Rehoboam
Abijah
Asa
Jehoshaphat
Jehoram
Uzziah
Jotham
Ahaz
Hezekiah
Manasseh
Amon
Josiah
Jeconiah
Jacob
Joseph — Mary
Jesus

Themes:

- Worship: If it's missing or just a ritual, spiritual death is just around the corner.
- God's faithfulness: God remained true to his covenants in the Old Testament and remains true to them today.
- God's justice: God had no other choice but to punish his people. God doesn't play favorites.
- Daily watchfulness: Israel and Judah never seemed to learn to be concerned for the present, and the result was their destruction. We can learn from their tragic examples.

Outline:

1 Chronicles	2 Chronicles
1–9: Family trees	1–9: Solomon's reign
10: Saul's reign	10: The kingdom divides
11–29: David's reign	11–36: The history and fall of Judah

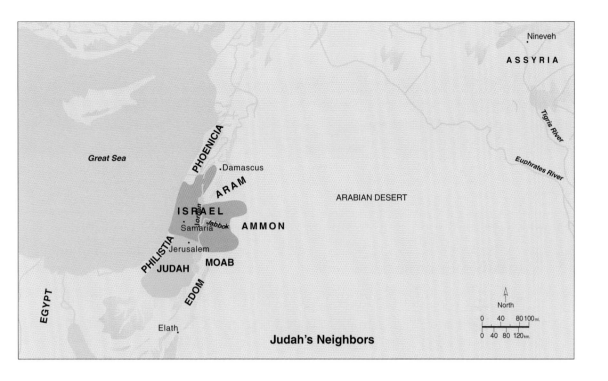

Judah's Neighbors

animals did not reproduce or became diseased. Judah's neighbors faced the same situation. The Canaanites responded to this precarious existence by worshiping gods who supposedly controlled rainfall and fertility. Although the people of Judah often flirted with Canaanite worship practices, God kept calling them back to the only secure life, the life found in their covenant relationship with him.

Judah's landlocked location also affected the people. The land of the Philistines lay between Judah and the Mediterranean Sea and kept Judah from becoming a seafaring country. Judah's lack of seaports probably kept out the luxury goods that the people would have enjoyed.

Desert sand separated Judah from Egypt. Because Egypt had become quite weak militarily, it was not Judah's primary enemy.

Some of Judah's neighbors were "family," but they weren't always friendly. The people of Ammon and Moab were descendants of Lot. The people of Edom, located southeast of Judah, were descendants of Esau. Together with Israel, they kept things active on Judah's borders.

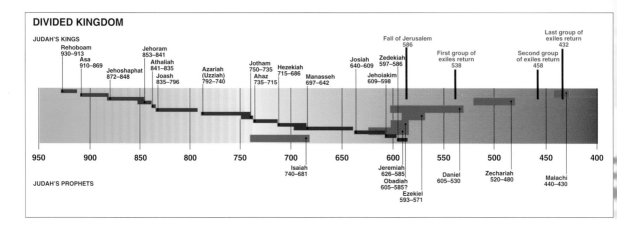

DIVIDED KINGDOM

JUDAH'S KINGS

Rehoboam 930–913
Asa 910–869
Jehoshaphat 872–848
Jehoram 853–841
Athaliah 841–835
Joash 835–796
Azariah (Uzziah) 792–740
Jotham 750–735
Ahaz 735–715
Hezekiah 715–686
Manasseh 697–642
Josiah 640–609
Zedekiah 597–586
Jehoiakim 609–598
Fall of Jerusalem 586
First group of exiles return 538
Second group of exiles return 458
Last group of exiles return 432

950 900 850 800 750 700 650 600 550 500 450 400

JUDAH'S PROPHETS

Isaiah 740–681
Jeremiah 626–585
Obadiah 605–585?
Ezekiel 593–571
Daniel 605–530
Zechariah 520–480
Malachi 440–430

Judah's Enemies

For many years both Aram and Assyria were threatening bullies. Assyria's war machine and Aram's cruelty created fear in the region. So Judah (like Israel) often joined with other small nations for protection.

By making alliances with pagan nations, the people of Judah opened themselves to invasion by pagan religions. Harmful religious practices snaked into Judah's worship. And the Baal worship that Jezebel brought to Israel also appealed to the people in Judah.

Turning from God's laws led to Judah's downfall. Every country that rejected God's laws experienced judgment. Assyria crushed Aram around 732 B.C. The Babylonians conquered the Assyrians in 608 B.C. and thus controlled the region that included Judah. The Babylonians under King Nebuchadnezzar destroyed Jerusalem in 586 B.C. Then Persians under Cyrus conquered Babylon in 538 B.C. Cyrus allowed the exiles to return to Jerusalem. During the reign of Darius, around 520 B.C., the returned exiles rebuilt the temple in Jerusalem.

2 ▬ ▬ ▬ ➤ Introduction to Psalm 33

Bible Reference: Psalm 33:12–22

Already this year you have learned or reviewed several Bible passages. Psalm 33:12–22 will remain with you as a beautiful record of God's promises to you and to a faithful community. It is also an example of Hebrew poetry. Paying special attention to the psalm's structure can be helpful in two ways. It can help you identify the covenant theme that connects with the other lessons in this unit, and it can help you memorize more effectively.

Hebrew Poetry

There's lots of poetry in the Bible. The third major section of the Old Testament contains books written mainly in poetic style. There's an epic poem (Job), a collection of hymns (Psalms), a collection of traditional wisdom (Proverbs), a meditation on life (Ecclesiastes), and a love poem (Song of Songs).

Hebrew poetry is different from English poetry. It uses special methods of repeating ideas (called parallelism) instead of devices such as rhyme. Here are three types of parallelism that the Hebrew poets used.

Similar (or rephrased): the two lines say almost the same thing.
"The chiefs of Edom will be terrified,
the leaders of Moab will be seized with trembling." (Psalm 55:5)

Contrasting: the second line states an opposite idea from the first line.
"Lazy hands make a man poor,
but diligent hands bring wealth." (Proverbs 10:4)

Completing (or amplified): the second line gives more details or adds a thought.
"For he will command his angels concerning you
to guard you in all your ways." (Psalm 91:11)

The Hebrew people loved to sing. Even their captors knew about their singing and asked for it (see Psalm 137:3). Many of the psalms were sung antiphonally—one group sang a phrase, and the other group sang the response.

You'll be reading this psalm at least two times in this lesson. The first reading will focus on the psalm's themes. The second reading will focus on its poetic structure.

Ask yourself the following questions before you read Psalm 33:12–22 for the first time. Look for the answers in the psalm.

- In this psalm, what is God's relationship with his people?
- What does it take to be a good king?
- What gives hope to God's people? What doesn't?

Before you read Psalm 33:12–22 again, think about these questions.

- Where does this passage contain examples of parallelism?
- What kinds of parallelism do you find in this psalm?
- How does the repetition strengthen the thought in verse 16? in verse 18?

Blessed is the nation whose God is the Lord,
   the people he chose for his inheritance.
From heaven the Lord looks down
   and sees all mankind;
from his dwelling place he watches
   all who live on earth—
he who forms the hearts of all,
   who considers everything they do.
No king is saved by the size of his army;
   no warrior escapes by his great strength.
A horse is a vain hope for deliverance;
   despite all its great strength it cannot save.
But the eyes of the Lord are on those who fear him,
   on those whose hope is in his unfailing love,
to deliver them from death
   and keep them alive in famine.

We wait in hope for the Lord;
   he is our help and our shield.
In him our hearts rejoice,
   for we trust in his holy name.
May your unfailing love rest upon us, O Lord,
   even as we put our hope in you.

Psalm 33:12–22

3 ▬ ▬ ▬ ▬ ▬ ➤ A House Divided—
Rehoboam the Proud

> Bible Reference: 2 Chronicles 10:1–11:4;
> 2 Chronicles 11:13–17; 2 Chronicles 12:1–12;
> Deuteronomy 17:14–20

In the last unit we traced the decline and destruction of the nation of Israel. Now we are going to go back and trace the story of Judah, the southern kingdom.

You remember that Solomon set the stage for the breakup of the kingdom. For one thing, he got carried away by his wealth and power and imposed harsh taxes on the people. He even forced some of his own people to work on his extravagant building projects. But even worse, he turned away from God in worship. Because Solomon broke his promise to God and worshiped idols, God judged him.

The prophet Ahijah announced that the kingdom would be torn from Solomon and his family. Ahijah took his new cloak and tore it into 12 pieces. He gave 10 pieces to Jeroboam, a rebellious government official, and he kept two pieces as a symbol that God would keep his promise to David. Even though Judah would become smaller and weaker because of Solomon's sin, God would keep David's family alive so that the promise of a messiah could be fulfilled.

Throughout the history of the kings of Judah, God used prophets such as Ahijah to remind his people of the covenant promises made on Mount Sinai. Rehoboam was given the choice to obey or disobey the covenant's terms.

Read about Rehoboam's decisions. Was he like his father? Watch for another prophet and his message, the king's response, signs of judgment, and signs of hope.

A Greedy King
(or How to Lose a Kingdom in One Easy Step)

Narrator 1: It's hard to tell exactly what Jeroboam was up to. Did he really care about the poor people who had to pay high taxes, or was he just trying to make trouble so that he could seize power?

Jeroboam (grumbling and complaining): Your father put a heavy yoke on us, but now lighten the harsh labor and the heavy yoke he put on us, and we will serve you.

Rehoboam: Come back to me in three days.

Rehoboam (turning to old advisor): How would you advise me to answer these people?

Old Advisor: If you will be kind to these people and give them a favorable answer, they will always be your servants.

Narrator 1: Rehoboam didn't like the advice of the old advisors and decided to consult some younger ones who had grown up with him.

Rehoboam (to young advisors): What is your advice? How should we answer these people who say to me, "Lighten the yoke your father put on us"?

Young Advisor 1: Tell the people who have said to you, "Your father put a heavy yoke on us, but make our yoke lighter"—tell them . . .

Young Advisor 2: My little finger is thicker than my father's waist.

Young Advisor 3: My father laid on you a heavy yoke; I will make it even heavier.

Young Advisor 4: My father scourged you whips; I will scourge you with metal-spiked whips.

Narrator: Three days later Jeroboam and all the people returned to Rehoboam, just as the king had told them to do. Rehoboam answered them harshly. Rejecting the advice of the old advisors, he followed the young men's advice.

Rehoboam: My father made your yoke heavy; I will make it even heavier. My father scourged you with whips; I will scourge you with metal-spiked whips.

Narrator: When all Israel saw that the king refused to listen to them, they answered the king.

Israelite 1: What share do we have in David, what part in Jesse's son?

Israelite 2: To your tents, O Israel! Look after your own house, O David!

Narrator 1: So all the Israelites went home, and the house of Israel has been in rebellion against the house of David to this day.

Narrator 2: Rehoboam did not take this sitting down! He gathered a fighting force of 180 thousand fighting men to make war against Israel and to regain the kingdom.

Narrator 1: But God spoke to the prophet Shemaiah and gave him a message for Rehoboam and all the Israelites in Judah and Benjamin.

Shemaiah: This is what the Lord says: "Do not go up to fight against your brothers. Go home every one of you, for this is my doing."

Narrator 1: So they obeyed the words of the Lord and turned back from marching against Jeroboam.

4 ➝ Rehoboam the Penitent

Bible Reference: 2 Chronicles 11:5–17

There was hope for Rehoboam! He obeyed God's prophet and abandoned his threat of retaliation against Jeroboam. For three years Rehoboam followed God's way and created a place where faithful priests and Levites from Israel came to worship. Judah grew strong and prospered. Knowing a bit about Rehoboam, do you think he kept up the good work?

Keep your eye on God in this lesson. Pay careful attention to his word spoken through the prophet. Notice God's response to a repentant heart, and try to discover what God wants for his children.

What it would be like if we were judged only on the basis of one or two incidents in our life? On what basis are we judged? What is the source of our hope?

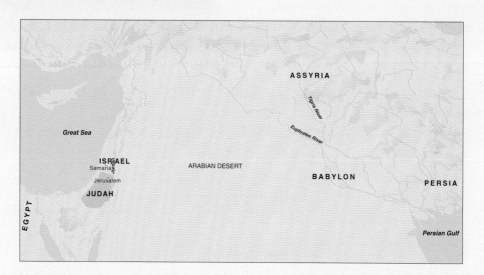

J udah was a tiny country located on the route between competing empires. Along
with its sister, Israel, Judah often suffered when armies from Egypt and the
empires of Assyria, Babylon, and Persia swept through the Palestine corridor. During
Rehoboam's time, Shishak, the king of Egypt, threatened his neighbors.

The empires of Assyria, Babylon, and Egypt were fighting to the death for power and
territory. In the process they ground the life out of smaller, weaker nations that stood
in their way.

God wanted his people to respond to him with loving trust. Sometimes Judah turned
from God's voice and arrogantly flirted with other gods and sources of security. God
used the raging empires to discipline Judah and call his people back to him.

5 − − − → A Matter of the Heart

> **Bible Reference: 2 Chronicles 13–16;
> 1 Kings 15:1–5**

Sometimes the stories of the kings and prophets seem unrelated to our
lives. The people of Judah and Israel were often tempted to worship something else important in their lives rather than God.

In both Kings and Chronicles the writers refer to the heart when they explain the spiritual history of the kings of Judah. The kings' hearts were of great importance to God. Sometimes they served God with all their hearts and practiced true, godly leadership. When their hearts were directed toward God, the people were blessed.

God is always the main character in the story of his people. In this lesson we hear God's voice through the prophets. They try to keep the people's hearts in the right place.

Two other characters are Abijah and Asa, kings of Judah. Abijah was the son of Rehoboam. The writer of the Book of Kings saw that Abijah was a king with a divided heart. King Asa had a heart that was committed to the Lord, but he had a few problems, too, especially with his feet.

Worship Undivided

During the time of the kings, it was difficult for the people to know God, and it was tempting for them to worship something that they could touch and feel. Although it seems strange to us now, the rituals and practices of the Canaanites made some sense to them.

The people living in Palestine depended on the rain and fertile soil for life. If rain was scarce and plants did not grow, people died of starvation. Maybe the people's temptation to serve the Canaanite rain and fertility gods

Objects found in a Canaanite temple.

is not so hard to understand. They thought that their very survival was at stake.

God wanted the people to see that he was the source of all life and that fertility was his good gift. God wanted the people to worship him—the Creator—not the things that he had created.

6 ━━ ➤ Jehoshaphat: Portrait of a Hero

> **Bible Reference: 2 Chronicles 17–20**

We've seen a pattern in the lessons of the kings and prophets of Judah. When the people sinned and broke the terms of the covenant, they were judged. Looking only at the judgment part of the story, it can be pretty discouraging, but the story tells about more than punishment. This story also contains a big "and." God's grace and mercy always go along with judgment.

In this lesson we are going to learn more about Jehoshaphat. He was an unusually good king, and God blessed him with peace and security. But even Jehoshaphat headed in the wrong direction sometimes. It took at least three prophets to keep him going the right way. Because Jehoshaphat accepted the prophets' guidance, God blessed him with vision and wisdom.

The Law and the Prophets

How would you like to live at school? You might not think that sounds like fun, but prophets lived together in schools during the time of the kings.

The prophets were ready to provide advice to the kings when they were making important decisions. The kings liked to check with prophets like Elijah before big battles. They wanted to know whether they would win or lose. True prophets like Elijah told the kings what God thought of their plans.

The prophets used God's law to evaluate the actions of the kings and the people. A copy of the law was kept in the ark of the covenant. The ark was considered most holy, the place where God's voice was recorded.

The prophets' "sermons" had three main themes. The first theme was that God's people were required to worship God alone, not idols. The second theme was that Judah would be judged for worshiping idols and oppressing the poor and powerless. The third theme was that people had cause for hope because of God's mercy showered on his repentant children. The sermons of the prophets pointed to Jesus, our Messiah and the source of life.

Jehoshaphat was able to create an orderly legal system and organize Judah's religious life.

As long as the kings and the people were heading down the right path, with their hearts tuned to his law, God was full of compassion and forgiveness. That's where we get our comfort, too. Our sins do not define us. God promises forgiveness for those whose repentant hearts long for goodness.

Read about King Jehoshaphat and notice these four things:

- The prophets guiding him
- His concern for faithful worship
- His love for the law and justice
- His walk of trust and faith

7 ━ ━ ━ ━ ━ ━ ➤ Hard Times for David's Family Tree

Bible Reference: 2 Chronicles 21–25; 2 Kings 9:1–7, 23–28

In the last lesson we thought about the law's function in society. God gave law so that people could live in harmony with him and with each other.

In this lesson we are going to look at the way five of Judah's rulers responded to God's law. We'll see how the evils of idol worship sickened the kingdom, but we'll also see evidence of God's mercy and faithfulness to his children. The kings and the people were unable to completely obey the law even when they, like Jehoshaphat, turned their faces and hearts toward God. We'll be reminded that as the people of Judah had to rely on God's covenant promise to David, we too can rely on Jesus, the fulfillment of that promise. Jesus is the light of the world, the lamp that will never go out.

Have you ever seen a fresh, green shoot growing from a dead-looking tree stump? In this lesson only one small shoot of Jesus' family tree survives. The tree is hacked back, not just trimmed or even pruned. Yet in the

For thousands of years people in Palestine used oil lamps to light the dark corners of their houses in daytime, and they used them everywhere at night. Archaeologists think that at first thrifty housewives used the bases of broken jars for lamps. They filled these jar fragments with olive oil and then draped a wick of flax or wool over the side.

By the time of Abraham, Isaac, and Jacob people took a more artistic approach to their lamps. They decorated the lamps with flowers or scenes from daily life.

Cautious housekeepers placed the lamps in little nooks and crannies of the walls to keep them safe from careless hands and feet. They tended the lamps with care because they didn't have matches to light them if they went out.

For the people of Judah, light became a symbol of the promised messiah, the light of the world.

Lamps from an ancient pottery dump.

person of young Joash, God preserved a tiny shoot of the family of David so that his promise of a messiah could come to pass for all people.

When you read about Jehoram, Ahaziah, and Athaliah, watch for God fulfilling his promise to David in the middle of a dark and terrible time. When you read about Joash and Amaziah, see the pattern of blessing and judgment take shape.

8 ⟶ Pride, Punishment, and Mercy

Bible Reference: 2 Chronicles 26–28

People used to say that a proud person had a "big head." In the American West, an arrogant person was described as being "too big for his britches." Every culture and probably every school has special ways to describe proud people. Many cultures create stories intended to warn children about the dangers of pride. Early church leaders called pride a deadly sin. The Old Testament is filled with references to the danger of pride.

The writer of the Book of James suggests that the one thing that should give us pride is our identity as children of God. Through the prophets God

Leprosy

Moldy, scabby splotches on the wall; spots on clothing caused by rot or fungus; and diseased, light patches of skin all had the same name in Bible times—leprosy. A person with crusty, lightened patches of skin was labeled a leper and was forced to leave the community. At the end of a complex process, the priest would declare the sufferer clean and purified before he was allowed to rejoin his family.

Because everyone was so afraid of getting that dreadful, disfiguring disease, town authorities sometimes forced lepers to shake rattles and to call out, "Unclean, unclean." People had good reason to be afraid. Untreated leprosy could result in the loss of a finger, a foot, or even a nose.

Today leprosy still exists, mostly in warm, humid climates. It can be treated, controlled, and cured. In most places people with leprosy are no longer isolated.

During the Old Testament times, the term leprosy was linked with impurity. For the people it symbolized more than just physical sickness. It represented moral disease and sinfulness.

King Uzziah received the mark of leprosy on his forehead. Early Christians received the mark of the cross on their foreheads.

kept reminding the people of Judah exactly what it meant to be the people of God. In the stories of the kings we, too, are reminded of our identity.

Some of the kings responded with joy and obedience to God's reminders of their true identity. Others rebelled. Yet God's mercy shines through over and over again.

In this lesson one king started out well, but God punished him with leprosy because of his pride and disobedience. The next king was so good that he might remind you of Jesus. The last king in this lesson will probably remind you of Queen Athaliah, a "moral leper." Although the story is filled with loathsome evil, it also contains a beautiful story of mercy and healing.

Background

When Uzziah began to rule, Judah was in a good position economically and politically. Damascus, the capital city of Aram, was under Assyria's control, and internal quarreling kept Assyria out of Judah's business. But things began to change during Jotham's reign. Under Tiglath-Pileser Assyria became powerful and again tried to dominate the surrounding countries.

This is Straight Street in Damascus, looking toward the East Gate and the houses built over the wall.

The people in Judah were afraid. Around 734 B.C. King Pekah of Israel threatened Judah. King Ahaz of Judah made an alliance with Assyria. The Assyrians destroyed Israel but eventually caused trouble for Judah as well. Before long until Judah became subject to Assyria. Fear and unrest led to religious unrest. Under Ahaz, Judah began to worship idols instead of God. When you read the story of Uzziah, Jotham, and Ahaz ask:

• Who were the lepers?
• What kinds of leprosy did they suffer?
• What kind of leprosy is most damaging?

9 ▬ ▬ ▬ ▬ ➤ Signs and Wonders

Bible Reference: Isaiah 7; 8:5–8, 13–15; 9:1–2

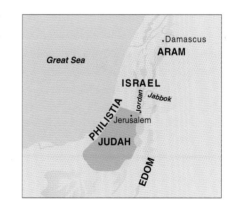

In this lesson we find Judah in another tough spot. Aram and Israel were threatening Judah because King Ahaz had refused to form an alliance with them against Assyria. Edom and Philistia were also attacking. God sent the prophet Isaiah to encourage Ahaz to rely on God. But Ahaz refused to listen, and judgment followed.

This lesson will introduce you to the prophet Isaiah as he tells the story of Ahaz. You will see his vivid images of judgment. He even used his own children as signs and symbols from God. Contrast Isaiah with Ahaz, who also used his children for religious purposes. What a difference!

This lesson has another sign, one of hope. And it isn't only for Ahaz in his time of trouble. Immanuel is a sign of hope for all God's people. The prophecy of Immanuel foreshadows Jesus' coming to live among his people. Jesus is truly "God with us."

Imagine what it might have been like to be threatened on every side. Can you understand Ahaz's decision to turn to Assyria for help?

Ask yourself who and what you rely on for courage when "enemies" surround you.

Honey

Your parents have probably called you "honey," an affectionate term for a loved one. In the Bible passage for this lesson Isaiah uses honey and bees to help us understand God. Our understanding of God is limited, but because God wants us to know and love him, the Bible gives us many different images of God.

In Bible times honey sometimes symbolized the sweetness of God's words and his law. At other times it symbolized abundance, having more than enough. The poor, wandering Israelites called Canaan a land flowing with milk and honey. Today we would be more likely to describe the Promised Land as flowing with pop and pizza.

Isaiah asks us to think of honey a little differently. Honey is the food of nomads. The people of Judah would soon need it, because they would be driven from their land. God, the beekeeper, was going to punish Judah with his bees, the Assyrians. Imagine God as a beekeeper whistling for his bees; as they streak toward him, he sends them off to sting evildoers.

Unit 5
Judah Is Judged

1 ━ ━ ━ ━ ━ ━ ━ ➤ The Message

Bible Reference: Isaiah 55:1–7

When the Jewish exiles were trudging the 800 long miles to Babylon, their deepest longing was probably to go home to Jerusalem. But as they entered Babylon through the royal blue Ishtar gate, they were surprised. They saw a prosperous city bustling with business activity. Exotic flowers and fruits grew abundantly. The tolerance of the Babylonian citizens was even more remarkable. At times the Babylonians even treated the exiles well. Babylon wasn't so bad after all.

Babylon's Hanging Gardens

A well-traveled Greek would try to see the seven man-made wonders. We call these the Seven Wonders of the Ancient World. One of these was a magnificent hanging garden on the banks of the Euphrates River in Babylon. An ancient source says that King Nebuchadnezzar had the gardens built after he married a foreign princess. He hoped that the lush gardens would make her feel at home.

Wide marble staircases connected terraces filled with exotic fruit trees and flowers. An elaborate watering system kept the plants blooming and the fountains bubbling. Artists have imagined lilies floating on reflecting ponds and princesses delighting in the delicacies of the gardens.

Isaiah may have foreseen a time when life in Babylon would be attractive to God's people. And so, in Isaiah 55 he called the people to return home to God. We can almost hear him calling like a hot dog vendor at a baseball game, "Come and get it!"

Of course, Isaiah's vision was always longer and wider than Judah's immediate story. His vision swept through the ages to the time of fulfillment, when the messiah would come. Isaiah's message stretches even to us today, and Babylon represents all the things that lure us away from God. Isaiah shouts, "Come away from the wonders of your world. Come and get the food that really satisfies, the Bread of Life, the Christ." But Isaiah does more than invite us to eat well. He also invites us to turn on our lights so that the people around us can see the way to Christ.

2 ▬ ▬ ▬ ➡ The Holy One of Israel

Bible Reference: The Book of Isaiah

It's hard to imagine what life was like before the time of radio, television, computers, and the Internet. Before the age of technology, people communicated by speaking face to face. Most people in Judah and Israel were illiterate. Only the elite could read and write. A person who could speak eloquently became the local newscaster and probably the local entertainment. Public speakers were important figures.

Prophets were the voice of God. Some scholars think that the prophet Isaiah was the most gifted writer and orator of the Old Testament. Crowds gathered to hear his vivid, colorful prophecies. In one of his messages Isaiah depicted God as a beekeeper and the Assyrians as a razor. He was trying to teach the people that Assyria would strip Egypt of its power and that it was foolish for Judah to put their trust in help from the Egyptians. Isaiah used powerful images to teach the people about trust in God, faithful worship, and God-honoring human relationships.

Isaiah

Who was Isaiah?

Family: His father was Amoz; he was married and had at least two sons.

Occupation: Prophet to Judah; sometimes called "world's first evangelist."

Career: Called in the year King Uzziah died (c. 740 B.C.); spent most of his life in Jerusalem; possibly killed by King Manasseh (c. 690 B.C.). Contemporaries: Amos, Hosea, and Micah.

The Book of Isaiah:

- Old Testament book most frequently quoted in New Testament and most frequently used by Jesus.

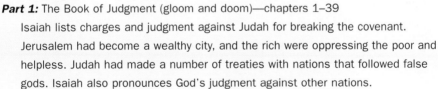

Isaiah by Gustave Doré.

- One of the best known and most popular books of the Old Testament because it contains many memorable verses.

- In a way it represents the whole Bible: the first part has 39 chapters (the same number as books in the Old Testament); these chapters are more immediate and historical, like the Old Testament. The second part has 27 chapters (the same number as the books of the New Testament); these chapters are more prophetic and spiritual, just as the New Testament is more evangelistic than the Old Testament.

Part 1: The Book of Judgment (gloom and doom)—chapters 1–39

Isaiah lists charges and judgment against Judah for breaking the covenant. Jerusalem had become a wealthy city, and the rich were oppressing the poor and helpless. Judah had made a number of treaties with nations that followed false gods. Isaiah also pronounces God's judgment against other nations.

Part 2: The Book of Comfort (hope and glory)—chapters 40–66

Isaiah gives hope and comfort for the exiles of Judah in Babylon, messages of warning to the returned exiles, and messages of future blessings and comfort for Judah and us.

Themes

- The holiness of God (he is called "The Holy One of Israel").
- God's control over all that goes on in the world.
- The coming of the Messiah, God's Servant.

The Historical Setting

To understand Isaiah's message it is helpful to know a little about the times when he prophesied. His ministry probably began during Uzziah's reign. At that time, Judah was nearly as rich and powerful as it had been during King Solomon's reign. Worship and sacrifice were regular and dramatic. Judah's future seemed secure. But it faced two big threats, an external one and an internal one. Assyria, quiet for many years, was now growling for conquest. Internal corruption also threatened Judah. Some people grew rich because they paid low wages and kept the people poor. Judges were corrupt. And the leaders assumed that offering lavish public sacrifices somehow made up for their sins.

The Structure of the Book of Isaiah

The first 35 chapters of Isaiah contain many prophecies of judgment. Isaiah prophesied that Assyria would brutally punish Judah. But sprinkled among the visions of doom are images of hope and restoration.

Chapters 36–39 tell the story of Jerusalem's miraculous deliverance from the Assyrians during the time of Hezekiah. This section ends with the gloomy prediction of Judah's fall and exile in Babylon.

The last section of the Book of Isaiah is filled with visions of restoration and comfort. Isaiah prophesied that God would restore his people after the terrible time of exile in Babylon. But Isaiah's prophecies extended beyond Judah to a time when all the earth would see the salvation of God. Through the work of Jesus, the suffering servant, we are drawn into God's long-ago promise to David. Isaiah had a vision of a light shining out to the whole world. God had a plan to restore the people of Israel and the Gentiles too. The light was shining for us.

3 — — ➡ The Song of the Vineyard

Bible Reference: Isaiah 5:1–7; John 15:1–8

Remember the Davidic covenant? It contained an unconditional promise to David. God promised that David's kingdom and throne would last forever (2 Samuel 7:16). The people of Judah were so secure in this promise that they forgot about the covenantal requirement to obey God's law. Isaiah reminded them that punishment from God was certain if they ignored their responsibilities to God.

Isaiah's Vineyard Song

The hillsides of Judah were dotted with vineyards. Isaiah was aware of this when he wrote the song of the vineyard. He knew that the people would understand what he was saying because vineyards were part of their lives.

What made a successful vineyard in Judah in Isaiah's day? One of the first and biggest jobs was clearing the land of rocks. (The soil all over Judah is still rocky.) Next, the farmer planted choice vines. After that, he built a watchtower, using many of the rocks cleared from the soil. The watchtower provided a shelter and a lookout point for the farmer while he guarded his vineyard from thieves and animals. Next, he dug out a winepress—a trough or small pit in the rock. When the ripe grapes were pressed, the grape juice flowed into this trough. Finally, a farmer who wanted the best possible vineyard would build a stone wall and plant a hedge around the vineyard for further protection. The hedge was usually a thick bush with sharp thorns.

Watchtower in Samaria.

Winepress at Capernaum.

The people of Judah needed to hear this. Most of them believed that God would protect them and bless them no matter what—no matter how they acted, no matter how they responded to the Lord, no matter how they treated the poor. Why? Because of God's covenant with David. Isaiah had a message for them. Isaiah had a song for them, and it wasn't a lullaby!

4 ▬ ▬ ▬ ➤ For to Us a Child Is Born

> **Bible Reference: Isaiah 9:1–7; 11:1–9;**
> **Hebrews 2:8b–18**

Building Trust

One of the most wonderful and frightening things that parents of toddlers experience is the complete, innocent trust of their children. A little child will jump off a sofa without warning, totally trusting that his parent will keep him from striking his head on the floor. When we get older, we're

Anointing

Prophets, priests, and kings were all anointed with oil because they were separated, or consecrated, for God's service. It was an offense to use holy anointing oil for common purposes (Exodus 30:22–33), and a person who had been anointed had to be obeyed (1 Samuel 24:6). People were consecrated by anointing because it was believed that the oil was from God and because oil made a person's hair and skin look their best. Anointing was also associated with the outpouring of the Spirit.

The Hebrew word for the anointed one is *mashiach* (messiah). Jesus combined the tasks of the prophet (who spoke to people from God), the priest (who represented the people before God), and the king (who established God's law) to become our mashiach to die for our sins. Jesus said that the spirit of God was upon him because the Lord had anointed him (Isaiah 61:1; Luke 4:16–21).

a little more careful, but we still want to trust our loved ones and be protected by them.

We also want to trust our friends, but sometimes they betray us. We want to trust our heroes, but sometimes they turn out to be undesirable human beings. Our Heavenly Father says, "Trust me."

King Ahaz's nation was threatened by the people of Israel and the people of Aram. Isaiah came to him and said, "Trust God." Isaiah gave him the sign of Immanuel, but Ahaz found it difficult to trust "God with us." He trusted an ally, the Assyrians, whose power he could measure. Isaiah warned Ahaz that this ally would soon be his enemy and continued to encourage all of Judah to trust God.

Isaiah used other images and illustrations to describe the coming of the trustworthy messiah. This "anointed one" would be a descendant of David and a light to all those living in darkness. Isaiah's light was for the people of Judah and beyond. In this lesson we will discover more about this messiah and the kind of kingdom he brings.

The writer of the Book of Hebrews gives the messiah another title—*brother*. He became like us. Jesus took our punishment and brought us into the family of God. Through Christ we too are God's children. Our Heavenly Father is waiting for us to jump into his arms. He will never drop us.

Ready for Action

Isaiah 11:5 says, "Righteousness will be his belt." In Old and New Testament times the belt (or girdle) was one of the main pieces of clothing. It was made of leather or linen. Another essential piece of clothing was the tunic. Both men and women wore tunics—sack-like garments with a V-shaped opening for the head and slits for the arms. Women's tunics were ankle length, and men's were usually somewhat shorter. The tunic was made of wool, linen, or animal skin. When a man needed freedom to work or to run, he lifted the hem of his tunic and tucked it into his belt. This was called "girding up the loins," and this phrase became a metaphor for being prepared.

5 ➝ Comfort, Comfort My People

> Bible Reference: Selected verses from
> Isaiah 40–66

The Parts of the Book of Isaiah

The first 35 chapters of Isaiah contain many prophecies about the Assyrian judgment on Judah and the surrounding nations. This first section also includes beautiful prophecies of hope that use vivid poetic images. The next chapters tell the story of King Hezekiah and the Assyrians. Chapter 39 tells of a foolish act of King Hezekiah: he showed off all of Jerusalem's treasures to the Babylonian visitors, who undoubtedly reported the great treasure to Babylon's leaders. Hezekiah seemed to be inviting an invasion. Isaiah must have shaken his head in disbelief when he heard what had happened. He predicted that the Babylonians would invade Jerusalem and carry the people off into exile. About 100 years later this prophecy came true.

A Vision of Hope

Chapters 40–66 prophesy of the time after the exile. Some Bible scholars call Isaiah the "Book of Comfort." It colors the future with hope and fills it with encouragement for God's people. It assures them that they will be rescued from exile and will return to their homeland.

Isaiah saw the vision of a rescue mission that went beyond God's chosen people of Judah. In many of the Old Testament stories and prophecies we have seen hints that God was going to send a light to his people and to all the people of the earth. The messiah Isaiah pictured would rescue his people and save all the people of the earth.

6 ▬ ▬ ▬ ▬ ▬ ▬ ➤ Judah on Trial

Bible Reference: Selected verses from the Book of Micah

Getting caught doing something that you know is wrong is very embarrassing. Has it ever happened to you? It's especially humiliating if it happens at school. When you walk down the hall, you think that absolutely everyone is whispering about what you did. The worst part is facing your mom or dad with the truth. Their quiet "Why did you do it? You knew better!" might hurt worse than a fierce scolding.

Sometimes tenderly but often fiercely, the prophets spoke for God. They said to the people of Judah and Israel, "What were you thinking? You knew better." In this lesson we will meet the prophet Micah. His message was much like Isaiah's message, but it was shorter. Both prophets reminded the people of Judah that they knew a better way to worship and a better way to treat their fellow human beings. God had given the way to them when he had given the law to Moses.

The Background

Micah lived and prophesied during the time of Jotham, Ahaz, and Hezekiah. His ministry began during a time of peace and great prosperity, but the Assyrians were becoming more threatening. Like a dark thundercloud, their chariots rumbled ominously in the distance, growing closer as Judah's sins continued. During Micah's lifetime the Assyrians crushed and destroyed Israel and invaded Judah.

Micah saw the relationship between the sins of the people and the cruel Assyrian judgment to come. His message was often harsh. He described corrupt and greedy leaders as cannibals "who tear the skin from my people and the flesh from their bones; who eat my people's flesh, strip off their skin and break their bones in pieces; who chop them up like meat for the pan, like flesh for the pot" (Micah 3:2–3).

Micah prophesied more than sin and judgment. He also saw a coming time of peace and healing. Micah prophesied that out of Bethlehem would come one "whose origins are from of old, from ancient times" (Micah 5:2). This ancient one would shepherd his people, provide safety and security, and be their peace.

Micah used the image of a courtroom to present Judah's predicament. Like a guilty child before his parents, Judah was brought into God's court. Judah stood before God, ashamed and guilty. Fortunately for Judah, and for us, the sentence and punishment did not last forever.

Micah

Who was Micah? We don't know much about him except that he was from Moresheth, about 25 miles southwest of Jerusalem in southern Judah.

When did he prophesy? Sometime between 750 and 686 B.C., during the reigns of Jotham, Ahaz, and Hezekiah, kings of the southern kingdom of Judah—so he was prophesying at the same time as Isaiah (also in Judah) and Hosea (in the northern kingdom of Israel).

What did he prophesy? Micah spoke out against Judah's worship of false gods— who were thought to bring rain, good harvests, and success in battle when they were given the right amount of sacrifices—and their false worship of the righteous God—who was not pleased with their empty worship and injustice in the way they treated each other.

Did Micah see any hope? Yes, he saw signs of hope in two places: Jerusalem (would become religious focus for the world and source of peace and God's blessing) and Bethlehem (would be source of a ruler to bring hope to the whole world).

"What does the Lord require of you?
To act justly and to love mercy and to walk humbly with your God." (Micah 6:8)

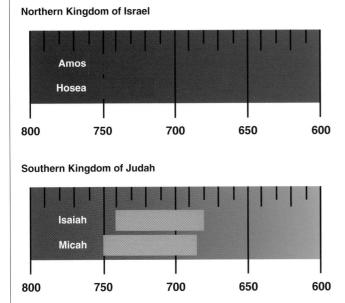

Northern Kingdom of Israel

800   750   700   650   600

Amos

Hosea

Southern Kingdom of Judah

800   750   700   650   600

Isaiah

Micah

Amos's Message
God is the ruler of history. He is righteous, patient, long-suffering, and impartial. He seeks fellowship with his people and demands righteous living. Israel's self-destructive sins will lead to God's judgment.

Hosea's Message
God's love for his people is steadfast, despite what they do. He takes the lead in dealing with his underserving people by extending grace and mercy to them. Israel must repent of their enormous sins before they can be renewed.

Isaiah's Message
Although God's promises to David are secure, God demands obedience to his laws and punishes disobedience. By punishing his people, God purifies them and clears the way for the fulfillment of the promises.

Micah's Message
God, who is righteous, hates idolatry, injustice, rebellion, and empty worship; he demands righteous actions from his people, not outward show. God delights in pardoning those who repent.

7 ------▶ The Day of the Lord

> Bible Reference: The Book of Joel

For most North Americans, a refrigerator without milk or a cupboard without chips defines catastrophe—especially after a hard day at work or school. The worst food related disaster that many of us can imagine is running out of our favorite snacks. Compared with people in developing nations, few of us really know hunger. Maybe you've heard someone claim that she will "just die" if she has to eat the same thing for dinner two days in a row.

If an Old Testament resident of Jerusalem said, "I'll just die if I have to look at another locust!" he wasn't complaining about having to eat fried or baked locust two days in a row. To the people of Judah, locusts were a plague and a curse, a natural disaster. When a cloud of locusts descended, death wasn't far behind.

Remember how God's people looked forward to the day of the Lord because they believed on that day God would put down their enemies once and for all? They were confident that God would judge and punish only the pagan nations. The people of Judah thought that their favored position with God protected and spared them from judgment.

Then the locusts invaded and devoured everything, including their grain and their grapevines. The people of Judah hadn't thought of themselves as targets of the Lord's judgment, but they were suddenly facing disaster. They needed to expand their understanding of the day of the Lord, so Joel set out to teach them.

In this lesson we will see how Joel's picture of the day of the Lord was bigger and better than the people of Judah had ever imagined. We'll also see how his vision benefits us.

Locusts

The Israelites probably wished they had something powerful and deadly to combat insects, because swarms of locusts could strip trees and vines of their leaves and even their bark in a matter of minutes. The locusts left tree branches white and dying and the people without food.

Locust invasions were unpredictable and deadly. Hot dry winds from the Arabian desert carried in swarms of the insect invaders. The females laid their eggs in tiny holes in the ground. When the larvae hatched, they devoured every plant in sight. When they developed wings, they were even worse. Huge, dark clouds of locusts swooped down on an even wider range of plants. The locusts devoured absolutely everything. It didn't take long for these marauders to consume a whole year's crop.

In small numbers however, locusts were not all bad. John the Baptist included them in his diet, and some people still consider them a delicacy. Some experts say that in the Bible the terms *grasshopper* and *locust* refer to the same creature, or at least the same type of insect. The people of Israel were allowed to eat insects that flew and hopped but not the crawlers. Their dinners could include a locust, katydid, cricket, or grasshopper. Yummm!

8 ━ ━ ━ ➤ Revival under Hezekiah

Bible Reference: 2 Chronicles 29–31:8

One of the most challenging aspects of growing up is figuring out who we are and how we fit in our families. When you get a good report card, your mom might greet you with a hug and tell you, "You're a chip off the old block." But if you accidentally hit a baseball through your grandpa's window, he might look annoyed and say, "Oh well, an apple doesn't fall far from the tree." For hundreds of years people have been compared to their parents in both favorable and unfavorable ways. Many people do not repeat their parents' mistakes, but many others do.

In this lesson we're going to leave the prophets and look at Judah's King Hezekiah. Hezekiah's father, Ahaz, had closed the temple and had led the people of Judah into worshiping Assyrian gods. He definitely was a "bad apple" or, at the very least, incredibly foolish.

Ahaz had invited the Assyrians into Palestine to protect Judah from Israel and Aram. Instead of leaving peacefully, the Assyrians made Judah a vassal state. Tiglath-Pileser demanded harsh tribute. Even worse, he

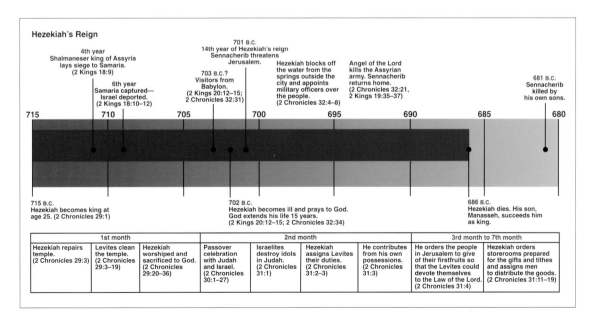

Judah's Bronze Snake

Snake worship was common in the pagan religions. Something like snake worship had also developed in Judah. Of course, the people had heard the story of the bronze snake in the wilderness many times (Numbers 21). Moses had made a bronze serpent and set it up on a pole, and all who looked at it were saved from the venom of the poisonous snakes in the camp. But now the people were bowing down and worshiping the

This head of Medusa with snakes for hair was found at the Temple of Apollo in Didyma.

snake on a pole. It no longer represented God's saving and healing power. The bronze snake had become an idol for the people of Judah. King Hezekiah ordered the snake destroyed along with the Asherah poles and sacred rocks.

demanded that the people of Judah worship Assyrian gods. King Ahaz did everything he could to appease the Assyrians. He even built an Assyrian altar where he sacrificed his own son.

By the time that Hezekiah became king, many of the people of Judah worshiped pagan gods, and Judah was squirming under Assyria's thumb. King Hezekiah knew that Israel had been destroyed because it had abandoned the covenant. He also knew that his father's religious practices and political decisions were leading Judah in the same disastrous direction. Fortunately for Judah, Hezekiah was not "a chip off the old block."

Hezekiah led Judah back to God. During his rule Judah experienced an incredible religious revival.

9 ━ ━ ➤ Like a Caged Bird

> Bible Reference: 2 Kings 18:9—19:37; Isaiah 36–38

A Difficult Situation

Imagine what it would be like if all travel and communication were cut off to and from your city: all planes, trains, cars, trucks, buses, telephone lines, computer connections, radio and TV transmitters. How long would the food supply last? How long would your city be able to survive on its own, cut off from the rest of the world?

This is exactly what happened to the people in Jerusalem when Hezekiah was king and Isaiah was his adviser. Around 705 B.C., when Sennacherib succeeded Sargon II as king of Assyria, King Hezekiah became a ringleader in a plot to overthrow the Assyrians. Before long Sennacherib's army mowed down the rebellious Phoenician and Philistine cities and then invaded Judah.

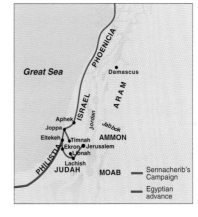

The news of the fall of Lachish—a powerful, well-fortified city—must have terrified the people of Jerusalem. They knew that it wouldn't be long until their nightmares about an Assyrian invasion would come true. Hezekiah's test of faith came in 701 B.C. when the Assyrians finally laid siege to Jerusalem. They sur-

Lachish viewed from the hill from which Sennacherib attacked.

rounded the city, cut off its food supplies, and waited for it to surrender. The following readers theater based on Isaiah 3:6–37 and other sources tells the story.

Under Siege

Narrator 1: Hezekiah had just received word that Assyria had attacked many Judean cities. He was worried. Lachish—a city he himself had fortified—had fallen. If Lachish had fallen, so could Jerusalem! So Hezekiah began to prepare for a siege. First, he sent for his chief engineers.

Hezekiah: We have a crisis on our hands. When Sennacherib arrives, I'm sure he'll surround the city and lay siege—like he did at Lachish. We have to be ready. First we must secure our water supply.

Engineer: My king, without the Gihon Spring, we have no reliable water supply, and you know the that Gihon Spring is outside the walls. Once we're surrounded, we won't be able to use it. What can we do?

Hezekiah: We must find a way to get the spring water inside the city. The only way is to build an underground tunnel from the spring, under the wall, and into the city. This way can we hide the Gihon Spring from Sennacherib and have a water supply.

Engineer: A tunnel? Why it would have to be . . . well, let's see . . . about 1,800 feet long!

Hezekiah (impatiently): It's difficult, but not impossible. It's the only way we'll survive!

Engineer: When should we start?

Hezekiah: Right now. Don't waste any time. Take as many men as you need, and work around the clock!

Narrator 2: The engineers formed two crews of workers. One crew started digging outside the wall at the spring, and the other started digging inside the wall near the king's garden. The idea was to meet somewhere in the middle. They worked feverishly. Some weeks later, the workers on one side could finally hear the workers on the other side banging against the rock. They called out; the other crew answered. They were about four feet from each other! Soon the tunnel was completed, and water flowed freely into the city.

Hezekiah's Tunnel

If a city under siege has food and ammunition and plenty of soldiers but is lacking one thing, it will not survive. What is that precious item? Water. When Hezekiah prepared for Sennacherib's siege, he wisely protected Jerusalem's water supply.

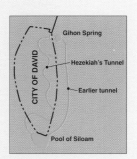

Hezekiah's tunnel, which was uncovered by archaeologists in 1880, follows a snake-like course beginning at the Gihon Spring, which is outside the city walls, and making its way to the southwest end of the City of David. There it feeds water into the upper pool of Siloam.

Hezekiah's tunnel.

Quarry workers cut the tunnel through the sheer rock ridge under the city so the water from the spring could flow through to a new pool built inside the city walls. Then the access to the spring from outside the city walls was blocked off. Two teams of quarrymen worked on the tunnel. One team started at the spring, and one team started at the pool. An inscription found inside the tunnel near the pool describes the moment that the two work teams met.

"While there were yet three cubits to be cut through, [there was heard] the voice of a man calling to his fellow, for there was an overlap in the rock on the right [and on the left]. And when the tunnel was driven through, the quarrymen hewed, each man toward his fellow, axe against axe. And the water flowed from the spring toward the reservoir for 1200 cubits, and the height of the rock above the heads of the quarrymen was 100 cubits."

If you visit the tunnel today, you can still see the pick marks of the quarrymen and identify the place where the two gangs met by the change in direction of the pick marks.

The Pool of Siloam.

Narrator 3: Meanwhile, Sennacherib, fresh from his victory at Lachish, was sure he could soon crush Jerusalem. He sent his field commander and a large army to Jerusalem to taunt and frighten the people. He thought that perhaps Hezekiah would surrender without a fight. Hezekiah sent three officials from his court to speak with the Assyrian commander.

Field Commander (loudly): Sennacherib wants to know why you Judeans think you can stand against us. You say you have strategy and military strength, but those are empty words. And if you think Egypt will help you, guess again. Egypt is like a splintered reed that only cuts your hand a bit if you lean on it!

Don't count on your God to rescue you either! After all, your king destroyed many of your God's high places and altars. How can your God be happy about that? Besides, he's the one who told us to march against this land and destroy it!

Palace Administrator: Please don't speak in Hebrew. All the people on the wall can hear you. Use Aramaic. We understand that language, and so do you.

Field Commander (loudly): Do you think my message is only for you? No! I'm speaking to the men sitting on the wall—who like you will have to eat their own filth and drink their own urine.

Narrator 1: The Assyrian commander was trying his best to intimidate the people of Jerusalem by describing what life would be like for them under siege—no food and no water. Then he turned away from Hezekiah's officials and spoke directly the citizens of Jerusalem on the wall.

Field Commander: Hear the words of Sennacherib, the great and mighty king of Assyria. Don't let Hezekiah lie to you. He can't save you. Your God can't save you. Make peace with me and come out to me. Surrender now, and each of you will eat from his own fig tree and his own grape vine, and drink from your own cistern. Later I'll take you to a land as rich as your own, full of grain and new wine, a land of bread and vineyards.

Narrator 2: The commander was trying to convince the people that loyalty to Hezekiah meant suffering and death but surrender to Sennacherib meant comfort and plenty to eat and drink. The people on the wall were silent because the king had ordered, "Do not answer him." When Hezekiah heard what the Assyrian commander had said, he tore his clothes, put on sackcloth, and went into the temple.

Hezekiah (to palace administrator): Put on sackcloth, and go to Isaiah. Tell him the words of the field commander, and ask him to pray for Jerusalem.

Narrator 1: The palace administrator, the secretary, and the leading priest all put on sackcloth and went to give Hezekiah's message to Isaiah.

Isaiah: Tell Hezekiah that this is what the Lord says: "Don't be afraid of the words of Sennacherib's commander. With these words he has blasphemed me. Listen! Sennacherib will receive a certain report, and when he hears it, he will withdraw to his own country. When he arrives there, I will have him cut down with the sword."

Narrator 3: Sennacherib received a report that the king of Egypt was marching out against him. He wanted to capture Jerusalem before taking on the Egyptians, so he quickly sent a letter to Hezekiah, urging him to surrender. In the letter he reminded Hezekiah that no army had been able to withstand the Assyrians. Hezekiah received the letter and read it. Then he went to the temple and spread it out before the Lord.

Hezekiah (in prayer): O Lord God almighty, God of Israel, you alone are God over all the kingdoms of the earth. Listen to the words that Sennacherib has sent to insult you. It's true, Lord, that the Assyrians have laid waste many peoples and have burnt their gods in the fire. But these were gods of wood and stone, made by human hands. Now, O Lord, deliver us from Sennacherib's hand, so that all the kingdoms on earth may know that you alone are God.

Narrator 1: Then Isaiah sent Hezekiah this message from the Lord:

Isaiah: This is what God says to Sennacherib: "Who is it you have insulted and blasphemed? Against whom have you raised your voice? Against the Holy One of Israel! Did you not know that I planned this long ago? You have conquered people and put them to shame. But I know where you stay, and when you come and go, and how you rage against me. I will put my hook in your nose and my bit in your mouth, and I will make you return by the way you came!"

This is what the Lord says to Hezekiah: "Sennacherib will not enter Jerusalem. He will not build a siege ramp against it. I will defend this city and save it, for my sake and for the sake of David, my servant."

Narrator 2: That night the angel of the Lord went out and put to death 185,000 men in the Assyrian camp. When the people got up the next morning—there were all the dead bodies! So Sennacherib broke camp and returned to Nineveh. There he bragged about his conquests and dictated glorious stories for his scribe to record.

Narrator 3: Not long afterwards, Sennacherib was assassinated by two of his sons.

10 ▬ ▬ ▬ ▬ ▬ ➤ Blended Religion

Bible Reference: 2 Kings 21; 2 Chronicles 33

In Whose Footsteps?

Manasseh became a king when he was only 12 years old. For the next ten years he ruled with his father, Hezekiah. As "apprentice king" he had time to learn how to rule Judah wisely, but he didn't learn from his father. As a child he had probably heard stories about the terrible destruction by the Assyrians. So Manasseh gave up his father's policy of resisting Assyria and willingly became a vassal of Assyria, just like his grandfather, Ahaz, had done.

Manasseh thought he had little choice. Only a few years after he became king, the Assyrians under Esarhaddon and Assurbanipal brutally crushed an Egyptian revolt. He probably figured that if Egypt couldn't stand up to Assyria, little Judah didn't have a chance.

Mixing It Up

Manasseh ruled as a vassal of Assyria for 55 years. Although there was peace as long as he was obedient to Assyria, Manasseh's policies had disastrous religious and spiritual consequences for Judah. As a vassal Manasseh bowed to the power of Assyria's army and also to its gods.

Manasseh built altars to the pagan Assyrian gods in the temple of the Lord. Magic, divination (using mediums to tell the future), and the worship of the sun, moon, and stars became popular in Judah. The people placed these beliefs and practices right alongside their belief in Yahweh. Sometimes they blended them all together.

This is the same thing that had happened in Israel. As you read the story of Manasseh, you will see many ways in which he was like Ahab. You will also see one significant difference. Manasseh found saving grace. But it was too late for the nation of Judah.

Next in Line

When Manasseh died, his son Amon took over. He ignored Manasseh's attempts to reform worship, and he encouraged Judah's pagan practices. God was not pleased with Amon's leadership, just as he wasn't pleased with most of Manasseh's reign. Amon lived for only two years, and then he was assassinated.

11 ━ ━ ━ ━ ━ ➤ Finding the Book

> Bible Reference: 2 Kings 22–23

Like a bully on the playground, Assyria threw its weight around. You probably remember some of the gruesome ways that Assyria controlled its vassals. When the Assyrians threatened to skin someone alive, they meant it; this was a standard technique.

But like all bullies, Assyria had a weakness. The empire had grown so large that keeping control was as frustrating as trying to stamp out a grass fire. You think that you have put it out at one end of the field when you

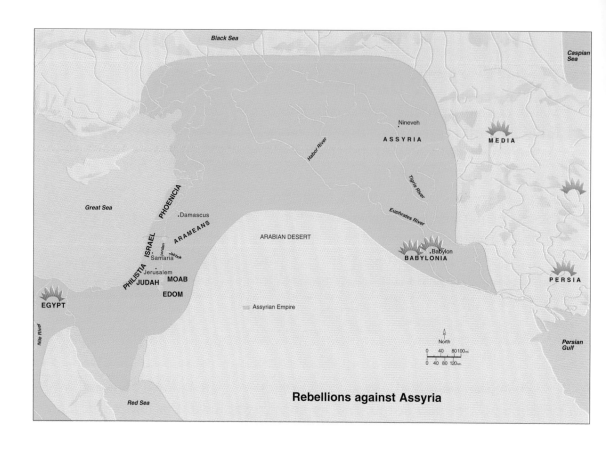

Rebellions against Assyria

spot a puff of smoke at the other end. That's what happened to Assyria. Rebellions blazed up all over the empire, but the ones in Egypt and Babylon were especially strong and stubborn. In 652 B.C. the Babylonians launched a major rebellion that took about four years for the Assyrians to stamp out.

Fighting the rebellions weakened the Assyrians. Barbarian tribes swooped down from the north and settled in what is now northwestern Iran. The Medes and Persians threatened from regions near the Persian Gulf and Caspian Sea. Before long the Babylonians rebelled again. Assyria's doom was not far off.

When Josiah became king around 640 B.C., Assyria was so weak that it didn't exert much control over Judah. Josiah's religious reforms were so complete that he destroyed an altar at Bethel that had existed since Jeroboam's time.

> *The Light of Israel will become a fire, their Holy One a flame; in a single day it will burn and consume his thorns and his briers.*
> *Isaiah 10:17*

D o you remember the story of the man from Judah whom God sent to Bethel to prophesy against Jeroboam's altar? He prophesied that someday human bones would be burned on that altar.

The day arrived when Josiah went to Bethel to clean out the tombs where the prophets of Baal were buried. As they were digging up those bones and throwing them on the altar fire, a certain tombstone caught Josiah's eye. One of the men of the city identified it as the tomb of the man of God who had prophesied the very things that Josiah was doing.

Needless to say, Josiah spared those bones. Read 1 Kings 13 for the rest of the story.

12 — — — — — → Assyria's Turn

Bible Reference: Nahum 1–3

A Popular Message

We often associate Old Testament prophets with bad rulers, not good ones. But during good King Josiah's reign several prophets were preaching God's message. In this lesson we will look at the prophet Nahum. Nahum was a prophet of doom to the Assyrians but a prophet of comfort to the people of Judah. He prophesied about the fall of Nineveh, the capital of Assyria. To the people of Judah who lived in terror of the Assyrians, this was welcome news!

They must have celebrated when Nahum said, "Do you remember what the Assyrians did to Thebes? Well, that's exactly what they are going to get!" Some of his listeners must have shuddered when they heard that part of the prophecy. Thebes wasn't the only place where the Assyrians had bashed the babies. Dozens of Judah's cities had been oppressed by the Assyrians during Hezekiah's time.

The Ultimate Weapon

The Assyrians knew the value of a secure water supply, and they designed channels to control the water into the city of Nineveh. The Babylonians were eager to get revenge for all of Assyria's cruelty, so they studied the fortifications of Nineveh carefully before they attacked.

The Babylonians discovered that it was possible to dam up the channels and restrict the supply of water to Nineveh. When the reservoirs were full, the Babylonians released the backed up water all at once. A raging wall of water tore away the foundation of the wall surrounding the city and caused large sections to collapse.

Nineveh did fall to the Babylonians in 612 B.C. The city was so completely destroyed that it has never been inhabited since. Within a few centuries it was covered by sand. No one even knew its location until 1845, when archaeologists discovered it.

Poetic Power

The Book of Nahum contains poetry with a punch. The poet-prophet packed vivid images into short phrases. Nahum painted a fearsome picture of the Babylonian army poised to plunder and destroy Nineveh, Assyria's capital city.

> The shields of his soldiers are red;
>> the warriors are clad in scarlet.
> The metal on the chariots flashes
>> on the day they are made ready;
>> the spears of pine are brandished.
> The chariots storm through the streets,
>> rushing back and forth through the squares.
> They look like flaming torches;
>> they dart about like lightning.
>
> Nahum 2:3–4

Now listen to Nahum's description of Assyria's sin.

> Woe to the city of blood,
> full of lies,
> full of plunder,
> never without victims!
> The crack of whips,
> the clatter of wheels,
> galloping horses
> and jolting chariots!
> Charging cavalry,
> flashing swords
> and glittering spears!
>
> Many casualties,
> piles of dead,
> bodies without number,
> people stumbling over the corpses.
>
> Nahum 3:1–3

Assyrian wall relief showing an Assyrian solder with a shield, spear, and helmet crest.

Vengeance

When someone elbows you when you're going for a rebound, what is your first instinct? Do you want revenge? When we think of getting revenge, we want to get even with someone.

The word *vengeance* occurs frequently in the Old Testament. When it refers to God, it has a different meaning. It is a legal term that means "righting wrongs." The Jewish people needed to be released from the extreme suffering caused by the Assyrians, and the poor and fatherless needed to released from oppression. Because God is righteous, he can't ignore evil. God isn't "getting even" with people; he is correcting the wrongs of sinful people.

Unit 6
Final Judgment

1 – – – – ➡ The Time Is Coming

"The days are coming," declares the Lord,
    "when I will raise up to David a righteous Branch,
a King who will reign wisely
    and do what is just and right in the land.
In his days Judah will be saved
    and Israel will live in safety.
This is the name by which he will be called:
    The Lord Our Righteousness."

Jeremiah 23:5–6

"This is the covenant I will make with the house of Israel
    after that time," declares the Lord.
"I will put my law in their minds
    and write it on their hearts.
I will be their God,
    and they will be my people.
No longer will a man teach his neighbor,
    or a man his brother, saying, 'Know the Lord,'
because they will all know me,
    from the least of them to the greatest," declares the Lord.
"For I will forgive their wickedness
    and will remember their sins no more."

Jeremiah 31:33–34

Though the fig tree does not bud
and there are no grapes on the vines,
though the olive crop fails
and the fields produce no food,
though there are no sheep in the pen
and no cattle in the stalls,
yet I will rejoice in the Lord,
I will be joyful in God my Savior.

Habakkuk 3:17–18

Yet this I call to mind
and therefore I have hope:
Because of the Lord's great love we are not consumed,
for his compassions never fail.
They are new every morning;
great is your faithfulness.
I say to myself, "The Lord is my portion;
therefore I will wait for him."
The Lord is good to those whose hope is in him,
to the one who seeks him;
it is good to wait quietly
for the salvation of the Lord.

Lamentations 3:21–26

2 ▬ ▬ ▬ ▬ ➤ The Day of the Lord, Zephaniah Style

> **Bible Reference: Zephaniah 1–3**

Imagine that the prophet Zephaniah has just finished a powerful sermon, and you have been invited to join a gathering of people who regularly get together after church to discuss the sermon. A wealthy worshiper hosts the gathering and serves the people rich, dark coffee and delicate almond pastries. As you wander around the room, cup in hand, you overhear many conversations. Some are angry, some are puzzling, and some you don't understand at all.

Narrator: Over in one corner the religious leaders sit together looking rather distressed.

Leader 1: I don't understand what he's got against astrology.

Leader 2: Yeah, right! It's not our fault that the Assyrians forced it on us.

Leader 3: And what's with that comment about my clothes! You'd think that being royalty himself he would know that the best fashion designers come from Nineveh. What's the big deal?

Leader 4: My kids think it's a game to hop over the threshold of the temple door. Do you think that's so bad?

Narrator: Is it so bad? you ask yourself, and then you move toward the business leaders and the money market experts. They are laughing together.

Leader 5: Doesn't everyone cut corners once in a while? Nobody needs to know that foreign kids made their athletic shoes. (*Snickers.*) We did make a pile on that little deal, didn't we. So what makes Zephaniah think that God will destroy us?

Leader 6: Aw, don't worry. Yahweh is no different from Molech or Baal. He won't do anything.

Leader 7: Well, I'm not worried. A little bribery goes a long way, no matter what Zephaniah says.

Leader 8: Hey, does anyone have a tent and a wine skin? (*The group laughs.*)

Zephaniah

Can you imagine the kind of courage it takes to walk away from a high-paying sports career in the NBA or the NHL? The prophet Zephaniah may not have been an athlete, but he likely had golden opportunities in King Josiah's court. Zephaniah's great-grandfather was none other than the famous King Hezekiah. He grew up in a royal family with all the privileges of education, wealth, and power.

Zephaniah was also exposed to all the corruption and pagan rituals that his grandfather Manasseh imposed on the people of Jerusalem. Yet God preserved him. That's what Zephaniah's name means: "The Lord protects." God used Zephaniah's noble training and education so that Zephaniah could speak to the the powerful leaders of Jerusalem with words and images that they could understand.

Zephaniah gave up his claim to the prestige and honor in the king's court to speak a message of judgment and hope.

Narrator: Their pride and cynicism is disturbing, so you move on to an earnest group of young princes.

Prince 1: I'm worried that Zephaniah came down so hard on us. I always thought that God was on our side. After all, he promised our father David that we would last forever.

Prince 2: It's clear that his day of the Lord is not just a bad weather day. It sounds like God is against us, not for us.

Prince 3: I'll tell you something. I don't want to be anyone's sacrifice.

Prince 4: I remember once when my great-grandfather was angry because our neighbors were worshiping the stars. He muttered something about remembering what Amos and Isaiah said. I guess we should be checking out what those guys said about the day of the Lord.

Narrator: As you move toward a group of foreign diplomats you remember what you learned about God's covenant with David and the requirements of the covenant given at Sinai. You wonder whether that old covenant stuff is important.

Diplomat 1: I don't suppose that this Zephaniah will make much of a difference. He says that our beautiful city will soon be the home of wild animals and screech owls. But just in case, I'm going to let my boss know what's happening. I'm sending a messenger today.

Diplomat 2: It sounds like Zephaniah has his

eyes on my country's best pasture land. I'm going to remind King Josiah that we have a treaty. They'd better not try anything funny. The "big boys" in Ashdod won't be happy.

Diplomat 3: Things have been going well for years. Now this prophet says that his God thinks we are proud and arrogant. We aren't insulting these people of God. We're just strong and confident.

Diplomat 4: I must say that I didn't like it when Zephaniah said that everyone in the world was in for his God's judgment. So we're all going to be burned up? His God doesn't have any control over us, for goodness sake. He isn't our God!

Narrator: As you move away, you so wonder whether these people's gods have only local authority. You wonder whether God's laws affect the whole world, even though many nations don't believe it. A commotion at the door interrupts your thoughts. Your gracious host is welcoming Zephaniah to the gathering. Zephaniah is talking earnestly, just as if his sermon never ended. You wonder why Zephaniah is so intense and why he insists on being heard. You listen intently to the prophet's conversation with the people around him.

Zephaniah: I wish that the day of the Lord's wrath would never come. If all these people in this room would just turn to God, they might find shelter. If only they weren't so proud and unjust, God's anger might turn away from them.

Listener 1: Oh, no. Here he goes again. I suppose he's going to call us greedy animals again and tell us to get righteous.

Listener 2: He's always preaching about righteousness—morning after morning, day after day. I'm sick of it!

Zephaniah: I knew you'd say that. You just don't get it, do you? This isn't just a hint; it's a warning, and I'll say it again—the whole earth will burn if you don't change.

Listener 3: I have a question. If we all deserve God's judgment, can we all receive God's mercy and healing?

Zephaniah: Why do you think God is cleansing the sin from the people of the earth? When the sin is gone and the meek and humble remain, they will be safe and secure. God delights in all those who rejoice in him. His love will be your comfort.

Narrator: Zephaniah leaves, and you sit in a corner quietly remembering his final words, "At that time I will gather you; at that time I will bring you home." You wonder when it will happen.

In Dagon's Doorway

One of the pagan superstitions the people of Jerusalem followed was hopping over the threshold of the door. This reflected an ancient superstition that probably began during the time of the prophet Samuel. When the Philistines captured the ark of the covenant, they placed it near a statue of their god, Dagon. The statue toppled over and broke, and Dagon's head rolled until it stopped on the threshold of the door.

Following that humiliating episode, Dagon's followers tried not to step on the threshold. They didn't want to anger Dagon by stepping on his head. By adopting this pagan custom, the people of Judah combined pagan practices with the true worship—making light of the covenant and all its requirements.

3 ──➤ Judah's Quick Downhill Slide

Bible Reference: 2 Kings 23–25

Zephaniah described the coming Babylonian invasion as terrible and unstoppable, causing panic and turmoil. The conditions in Judah mirrored those in Israel 100 years earlier when the people of Samaria faced Assyrian invasion. Do you remember how the rivalry led to assassinations and political chaos in Israel?

Following Josiah's death in 609 B.C. Judah was filled with conflicting political groups. Some were pro-Egypt, others were pro-Babylon, and still others opposed all foreign alliances. Selfish decisions by Judah's kings and political chaos led to the fall of Jerusalem in 587 B.C. Here's how it happened.

Egyptian Domination 609–605 B.C.

The Death of Josiah

During most of Josiah's reign Judah was not seriously threatened. But toward the end of his reign the international situation became shaky as two powerful nations challenged each other. The Babylonians were a major power after they destroyed the Assyrian capital of Nineveh in 612 B.C. Egypt, under Pharaoh Neco, was another major power. In order to control Babylonian expansion, Neco decided to join a last-ditch effort by the Assyrians to fight the Babylonians.

After listening to his advisors, Josiah committed Judah's army to Babylon. Josiah took his army to intercept the Egyptian army marching north along the Mediterranean Sea. It was a disastrous mistake. In a battle near Megiddo in 609 B.C. Judah's army slowed the Egyptians but didn't stop them. This ill-advised encounter cost Judah its king and Josiah his life.

Looking out the Megiddo gateway at the Esdraelon Plain.

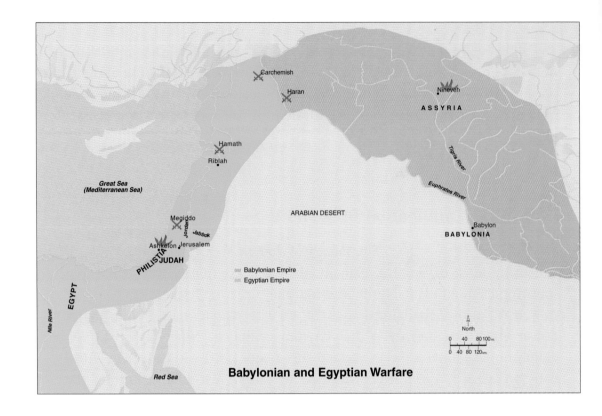

Babylonian and Egyptian Warfare

Battle at Haran

The Egyptians traveled northward to join the Assyrians at Haran. The Babylonians humiliated the Egypt-Assyria coalition in the battle there. In 609 B.C. the Assyrian Empire was demolished at last. The Euphrates River became the border between the two remaining powers. Babylon controlled the territory east of the Euphrates, and Egypt controlled the territory west of it—including Judah.

The people of Judah were restless vassals. To try to head off any pro-Babylon activities, Pharaoh Neco got rid of King Jehoahaz. He summoned Jehoahaz to his headquarters at Riblah, stripped him of his authority, and sent him off into exile in Egypt.

Pharaoh Neco then made Jehoiakim king and extracted heavy tribute from him. Of course Jehoiakim taxed his people to pay the tribute. He also wasted enormous amounts of money, time, and resources building himself a new palace. His foolish use of forced labor on the new palace created further stress in Judah. He was a poor excuse for a king and allowed the reforms of his father, Josiah, to die out.

Babylonian Domination 605–587 B.C.

The Babylonians Are Coming

Egyptian control of Judah didn't last long. In 605 B.C. the international scene changed drastically. The Babylonians—led by the brilliant young general Nebuchadnezzar—humiliated the Egyptians at the battle of Carchemish. The Babylonians relentlessly followed the retreating Egyptians to Hamath and crushed them there.

By the end of 604 B.C. the Babylonians had advanced south along the Mediterranean. Their destruction of the Philistine city of Ashkelon in 604 B.C. positioned the Babylonian army at Judah's doorstep. The threat threw Judah into a panic. Knowing that the weakened Egyptians could not save them, Judah's King Jehoiakim chose to become a vassal of Nebuchadnezzar.

Looking south at the Mediterranean Sea from the Ashkelon excavation.

But Jehoiakim kept waiting for an opportunity to slip out from under Babylon's thumb. He saw his chance when Nebuchadnezzar attacked the Egyptians in 601 B.C. and both armies suffered heavy losses. Jehoiakim saw this as a Babylonian defeat and decided to rebel. This was a bad mistake. By 598 B.C. the Babylonian forces returned to thrash the rebellious people of Judah. Jehoiakim died shortly before the Babylonian attack. Some think that his officials assassinated him, hoping to gain milder treatment from Babylon. In any case, his 18-year-old son Jehoiachin became king.

Within three months Jehoiachin surrendered to Nebuchadnezzar. It was 597 B.C. Nebuchadnezzar took Jehoiachin, his mother, his court officials and about 10,000 other captives to Babylon. The prisoners included all the fighting men and their officers, all the craftsmen, all the nobles, and the prophet Ezekiel.

The Last King of Judah

After he had put down this little rebellion, Nebuchadnezzar appointed Jehoiachin's uncle, Zedekiah, to take the throne in Jerusalem in 597 B.C. Zedekiah ruled during Judah's last 11 years. Major obstacles prevented Zedekiah from being an effective king. For one thing, powerful people kept pushing for another rebellion against Babylon, and Zedekiah found it difficult to resist them. He also faced opposition from people who remained loyal to Jehoiachin, the exiled king living in Babylon. Some experts think that the biggest problem was that Zedekiah was just plain wishy-washy. In any case, he was not able to stop Judah's destruction in 587 B.C.

4 ━ ━ ━ ➤ Asking Hard Questions

Bible Reference: The Book of Habakkuk

Does the following scene sound familiar? You are five or six years old, and it's about 6 o'clock in the evening. You have just kicked your younger brother and yelled at your older sister. Your mother looks carefully at your flushed cheeks and announces that it's bedtime for you. You react with anguish. "Why?" you howl. "My bedtime isn't for another hour." The cruel injustice is made worse when your brother sticks out his tongue and your sister giggles as you are firmly led off toward your bedroom.

With teary eyes you again demand, "Why?" Your mom explains that you look like you might be getting sick. She even takes your temperature. When you ask what will happen to your brother, she tells you that he will come to bed in a little while. You wail, "It's not fair! He's supposed to go to bed before me." She again tries to explain how important it is for you to get extra rest, and she assures you that you will feel better in the morning. As she kisses you one last time and turns out the light, she says, "Trust me. You'll be just fine."

> Though the fig tree does not bud
>> and there are no grapes on the vines,
> though the olive crop fails
>> and the fields produce no food,
> though there are no sheep in the pen
>> and no cattle in the stalls,
> yet I will rejoice in the Lord,
>> I will be joyful in God my Savior.
>>> Habakkuk 3:17–18

What's God Doing?

When you are upset because of what's going on in the world, turn to the words of the prophet Habakkuk. Habakkuk lived during King Jehoiakim's reign, and he noticed all the ways that the people of Judah were ignoring the covenant. It was hard for him to accept the promise that God would make things right. Habakkuk took his questions straight to God. His conversation with God takes up the first two chapters of the Book of Habakkuk.

We don't know what tone of voice Habakkuk used. But we do know that Habakkuk asked God how he could tolerate all the corruption and sin in Judah. When God told him of Judah's coming judgment at the hands of the Babylonians, Habakkuk's response was, "Wait a minute! That's not fair! The Babylonians are worse than we are. They're the ones that deserve to be punished."

God answered him again, this time by listing Babylon's sins and punishment in vivid detail. God reassured Habakkuk that the Babylonians would not get away with murder.

Habakkuk's reaction was awed silence. And then he prayed. The first part of his prayer is a plea to God to come and repeat his mighty acts of deliverance "in our day." The next part of his prayer celebrates those acts of deliverance. The last part of chapter 3 is Habakkuk's beautiful statement that even though God's people were suffering terrible devastation and loss, Habakkuk would still "be joyful in God my Savior."

5 — ➤ Jeremiah, a Teenage Prophet

> **Bible Reference: Selected passages from the Book of Jeremiah**

Imagine that it is one of those sunny, blue-sky days that sometimes follows a rainstorm. You and your brother are on your way to a neighboring town, and you are the first ones to discover that a bridge has been washed out. Your heart pounds as your brother's pickup truck skids to a stop. By

Jeremiah and His Message

Jeremiah by **Donatello, 1427.**

? Who was Jeremiah?

Jeremiah was born in the little town of Anathoth, which was located just north of Jerusalem. His father, Hilkiah, came from a priestly family that probably dated back to the time of Eli and the ark of the covenant at Shiloh. As a young boy Jeremiah must have wondered whether he would follow in the family tradition and become a priest. God let him know exactly what was in store. When Jeremiah was around 14 years old, the word of the Lord came to him, and his life was changed forever.

? How long was he a prophet?

Jeremiah was a prophet in Judah for at least 40 years, spanning the reigns of five kings. He began prophesying during Josiah's reign and continued until the fall of Jerusalem in 586 B.C.

? What was his message?

The foundation of Jeremiah's message was that God is the creator and ruler of everything; he knows human hearts, helps those who trust him, and demands that his people respond with faith and obedience. A second point Jeremiah stressed was human responsibility to God: we're all accountable for our actions, and we can't use outside factors as excuses for our wrongdoings. Jeremiah also urged Judah to trust in God alone, and he opposed the false religions and teachers of his day.

mere inches you avoid tumbling into the swollen, muddy river raging far below. After you have calmed down, you turn back toward town to warn other drivers. You wave frantically and shout, but no one stops. They speed past, probably thinking that you are a lunatic. You finally manage to slow some drivers down, but they glare at you impatiently as their cars squeeze between you and your brother. You feel sick as you realize that many of them will drown in the river, but you can do nothing more to save them.

The prophet Jeremiah was in a similar position. He tried to warn the people of Judah to turn from the path they were following, a path that led to their nation being wiped out by the Babylonians. For more than 40 years Jeremiah watched his people lurch from one disaster to another. And then, with deep sadness, he witnessed their final destruction. No matter how much he shouted and waved his hands, the people would not listen. He could not save them.

If the people had simply ignored Jeremiah, it would have been bad enough. But their hatred of his message and their hostility toward him made Jeremiah's situation even worse. When God called Jeremiah, he had warned him that his life was going to be tough. It was, but God never failed him.

6 ➜ The Unpopular Prophet

Bible Reference: Selected passages from The Book of Jeremiah

Most adults will admit to being at least somewhat concerned with popularity during their middle school and high school years. Many can name times when they sat home wishing the phone would ring or wishing that the mail had brought them an invitation. For many adults, memories of the "good old days" are not entirely good.

If you could talk with Jeremiah, what do you suppose he would say about his popularity in Judah back in the seventh century B.C.? One thing

Jeremiah accused the people of Judah of having a god for every town. The Canaanites had named the towns in honor of their gods long before God's people entered Canaan. Even Jeremiah's hometown, Anathoth, was named for a pagan goddess. She was the bloodthirsty goddess of war, Anat.

The city of Jericho was named for a moon god, Yareah. Four towns were called Beth-Shemesh, all named for the sun god, Shemesh.

Tel Jericho from the west.

is sure: Jeremiah probably wouldn't describe his teenage years as sweet. He was not considered the life of the party. In fact, his life and work often brought scorn and hostility. The fourteen-year-old Jeremiah must have been terrified when he was tapped on the shoulder by God. God handed Jeremiah a career that guaranteed mockery, persecution, and perpetual unpopularity—an offer that Jeremiah was not allowed to refuse.

In this lesson we're going to look at Jeremiah's message and try to discover the reason for his unpopularity. Like the prophets before him, Jeremiah evaluated the people of Judah on the basis of their response to God's covenant requirements. He asked the people questions such as, Who are you? What does your maker say? What's really important?

Even though it was difficult, Jeremiah never stopped asking questions, and he never sweetened his message for popularity's sake. How could he have been so strong?

7 ▬ ▬ ▬ ▬ ▬ ➤ Jeremiah's Trials

Bible Reference: Jeremiah 26–28, 32, 36–38

When you read the title of this section, perhaps you envisioned Jeremiah being hauled into court to face a judge and a jury. In part that's an accurate picture, because Jeremiah was accused in a court-like setting. But the word *trial* also means suffering and sorrow. Jeremiah's life was full of those kinds of trials. He suffered for speaking the truth and obeying God. Once the leaders of Judah even threw Jeremiah into a cistern, where he was kept for months without light, warmth, or adequate food. Why did they do this to Jeremiah?

Whenever a nation is threatened, people become fearful. Debate and opposition can be perceived as treason. After Josiah's death, the people of Judah were frightened by the Babylonians. When Jeremiah told them that a Babylonian victory was unavoidable, they called him a traitor. The leaders were counting on God to miraculously save them from the Babylonians, just as he had saved Jerusalem from the Assyrians. They wanted their prophets to be as upbeat and positive as Isaiah had been with King Hezekiah.

Jeremiah's political statements were not all that disturbed Jerusalem's leaders. Jeremiah announced that the Babylonian threat and the horrible spiritual condition of God's people were related. Jeremiah bluntly told them that God was sending the Babylonians to punish them for their sins. Judah's leaders did not want him to speak to the people about repentance or about surrender to the Babylonians, so they tried to silence Jeremiah by beating, starving, and imprisoning him.

Water was scarce in Judah and Israel, and the people collected rainwater in large reservoirs called *cisterns*. Families often had their own cisterns and cities stored community water supplies in cisterns that held thousands of gallons of water. Some experts say that large community cisterns held over a million gallons. People lowered buckets down the cistern's neck to the bulb-shaped chamber below. They lifted out cool, moderately clean water.

A cistern opening.

Judah's leaders jailed Jeremiah in a cold, muddy cistern perhaps 40 feet below the earth's surface. A kind Cushite official rescued Jeremiah. He used rags and old clothes to cushion Jeremiah's ride on a rope out of the cistern.

If you look carefully around the foundation of an old farmhouse, you might discover a damp cement cistern buried near a corner of the house. Few of these cisterns are used anymore, but at one time North American farmers collected rainwater them. Then they would not be without water if their wells failed.

Inside the Masada cistern.

8 ━ ━ ━ ━ ➡ Jeremiah's Laments

> **Bible Reference: Selected passages from Jeremiah 11–20**

Tali: Come on, Yaron. Our neighbor Michal told mother that the Babylonians have gone off toward Egypt. It's safe to go out and get water.

Yaron: Can't you go by yourself? I promised to meet my friend David today. We're going to the abandoned cistern to see if we can hear Jeremiah weeping and wailing.

Tali: Yaron, shame on you! You shouldn't make fun of him. Mother says he is the only true prophet in this city.

Yaron: It was wrong of me to say that. I'm really not making fun of Jeremiah. Actually he scares me a little. David said that he's really skinny, and his hair is long and dirty.

Tali: It makes me so angry when I think of what Pashhur is doing to Jeremiah. Pashhur is supposed to be a priest of God, but he's sure using cruel methods to shut Jeremiah up. Poor Jeremiah; that muddy cistern is so stinky and dark!

Yaron: Cousin Shaphan says that Jeremiah deserves to die. Shaphan even called him a traitor and a coward. He says that Jeremiah doesn't believe the lessons from the Holy Book.

Tali: What does Cousin Shaphan know? Jeremiah knows the stories better than anyone else!

Yaron: Shaphan said that if Jeremiah really trusted God, he would prophesy that the Babylonians will die just like the Assyrians did long ago. Instead he tells us to surrender to the Babylonians.

(Father enters.)

Father: What's the problem here, Tali? Why haven't you two left yet? The well will be dry if you two don't get going.

Tali: Yaron says that Jeremiah is a traitor, but I don't believe him. Do you remember when Jeremiah broke Shallum's beautiful clay pot? He had tears in his eyes when he told us that the Babylonians would break us just as easily. I just wish everyone could hear him talk. He sounds so sad when he tells us that there isn't any hope. He could never be a traitor.

Yaron: I didn't call him a traitor. I only said that people think he's a coward. I sure wouldn't want his job. I'll bet Jeremiah wishes that God had never made him a prophet.

Father: You'll have to ask him. Do you want to bring him a message for me?

Yaron: Were you eavesdropping, Father? You knew that I wanted to go to the cistern, didn't you!

Father (smiles): Go quickly, then. Stop at the cistern after you go to the well so that you can lower some water for the prophet along with this piece of bread.

Yaron: What shall we tell him?

Father: Tell Jeremiah to get ready for sunlight. God hasn't forgotten him, and neither have we. His friend Ebed-Melech is on the way to rescue him from the cistern. He has to move quickly before King Zedekiah changes his mind.

- If you were Jeremiah, would you want to switch careers?
- How do you think Jeremiah handled all the suffering that came his way?

> I am ridiculed all day long;
>   everyone mocks me.
> Whenever I speak, I cry out
>   proclaiming violence and destruction.
> So the word of the Lord has brought me
>   insult and reproach all day long.
> But if I say, "I will not mention him
>   or speak any more in his name,"
> his word is in my heart like a fire,
>   a fire shut up in my bones.
> I am weary of holding it in;
>   indeed, I cannot.
>
> **Jeremiah 20:7b–9**

9 ━ ━ ━ ━ ➤ Repent and Be Saved

Bible Reference: Selected passages from the Book of Jeremiah

If Jeremiah had lived today, he might have used the image of a faulty computer chip to describe God's straying, disobedient people. He used an image familiar to the people of Palestine—that of a broken pot. He bought a pot from a Jerusalem potter and then broke it dramatically, using a teaching method that the Egyptians had used over a thousand years before. An Egyptian potter would write the name of one of Egypt's enemies on a pot. Then an official would then hurl the pot to the ground, smashing it beyond repair. This act was a prediction and a threat.

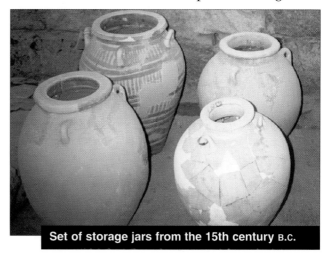

Set of storage jars from the 15th century B.C.

Jeremiah's goal was not the destruction of God's people. He desperately wanted the people of Judah to repent and turn to God so that they would not become a broken pot. Jeremiah got the people's attention, but their response was not what he wanted. Instead of changing their ways and turning to God, they labeled Jeremiah a crackpot. They thought Jeremiah was leading the country to disaster with crazy and dangerous ideas.

Before long the Babylonians did just as Jeremiah had prophesied. Judah was soon smashed beyond repair. In this lesson you will see the prophet not as a crackpot but as a man whose heart was breaking because the people stubbornly refused to listen to God's warning.

10 ━ ━ ━ ━ ━ ➤ A Story of Hope

Bible Reference: Jeremiah 32 and other
selected passages from Jeremiah

"I'll tell you a story." These were magical words when you were in kindergarten. Most young children—and many older ones too—love to be told a story. Even teachers can lose track of time when they are reading a story, and sometimes they can be persuaded to read another chapter.

One of the reasons that good stories survive is because they affect us at more than one level. Events, characters, and even the setting represent something else. They represent us and our difficulties and conflicts. And so we all heave a big sigh of relief each time we hear that Hansel and Gretel escaped, because it reassures us that we too will make it.

In this lesson the people of Jerusalem were facing annihilation. Their city was surrounded by a Babylonian army as fierce and terrible as the Assyrians had ever been. Jerusalem's destruction was only days away. Nebuchadnezzar was ready to crush the rebellious people of Judah once and for all. Their situation seemed hopeless, and then God gave them a story. This story was a precious gift to Jeremiah and to the people of Judah because it was more than just a story about a business transaction. It was a story of hope. The land that Jeremiah was instructed to buy was more than a plot of land belonging to his relative. It represented the Promised Land that God had given to his people.

As you read the story of Jeremiah's land deal, ask yourself why God would tell someone to buy real estate that was about to be conquered. What was God saying about the future?

Jeremiah Buys a Field and Wonders Why

Cast:	Crowd of Jewish people	Jeremiah
	Baruch	Messenger
	King Zedekiah	Jewish man
	Hanamel	Harim

Setting: the courtyard where Jeremiah is held prisoner

Crowd: You have company, Jeremiah. Look who's here. It's your friend Baruch!

Baruch: King Zedekiah is on his way to see you, Jeremiah. Are you going to tell him, "I told you so?"

Jeremiah: Perhaps that wouldn't be wise. Do you really think that I need to say anything to him? He knows that the end is near. This siege will have to end soon. I've heard that there aren't even any dogs or cats left to eat.

Baruch: What do you think the king is going to say?

Jeremiah: He'll probably ask the same questions again. At first he laughed when I told him that he would soon have a face-to-face meeting with the king of Babylon. Now he is terrified and wants me to tell him something good.

Messenger: Hear ye, hear ye, Judah's king, the honorable Zedekiah, approaches!

Crowd: Be careful what you say, Jeremiah. Remember the cistern!

Zedekiah: Hail, O prophet of God.

Jeremiah: Hail to you, O king.

Zedekiah: What word from God has come to you? Anything new?

Jeremiah: God's word has not changed. Read the scroll to the king again, Baruch.

Baruch: Here is the word of the Lord, O king. "'Zedekiah, king of Judah, will not escape out of the hands of the Babylonians, but will certainly be handed over to the king of Babylon and will speak with him face to face and see him with his own eyes. The king of Babylon will take Zedekiah to Babylon, where he will remain until I deal with him,' declares the Lord. 'If you fight against the Babylonians, you will not succeed. Your sons . . .'"

Jeremiah (*interrupts and whispers*): Stop there, Baruch. Don't read the part about his eyes.

Zedekiah: Isn't there any other word from God? Something hopeful?

Jeremiah: There is another word from the Lord, but I find it a little puzzling.

Messenger: Well, out with it, man! The king doesn't have all day!

Baruch: None of us have much time. Be patient!

Jeremiah: This is the word of the Lord that came to me. Make of it as you will. God told me this: "Hanamel, son of your uncle Shallum, is going to come to you and say, 'Buy my field at Anathoth, because as nearest relative it is your right and duty to buy it.'"

Jewish man: I'm no scholar, Jeremiah, but it sounds to me like the words of Moses. I think those words are in Leviticus somewhere. Didn't Moses tell us to keep land in the family? If your cousin shows up, I'm afraid you're stuck with a field in Anathoth.

Baruch: I don't understand why God wants you to buy land near Anathoth. It was your so called friends from Anathoth who plotted against you, Jeremiah. I think it was foolish for you to prepare a deed of sale. But I guess it's not for me to say.

King's man: Listen, here come some more visitors.

Baruch: They are dressed like the men of Anathoth, master.

(*Hanamel and his son Harim enter.*)

Crowd: Watch out, Jeremiah. This isn't the first time the men of Anathoth have visited you.

Jeremiah: Why, it's my cousin Hanamel and his son Harim, just as the Lord said. Greetings. We have nothing to offer you except for a cup of water and a place in the shade. Rest yourself. You have had a long journey. What's on your mind?

Hanamel: You are most wise, cousin. Everyone tells of your great relationship with God and your concern for . . .

Jeremiah (interrupting): You don't need to flatter me, Hanamel. What's your concern?

Hanamel: I can't pay the taxes on my field near Anathoth, cousin. Will you buy it? I'll give you a good deal. You know that it's your right and duty to redeem our land. And we all know that you honor and obey God's law.

Baruch: Why should my master help you out after all you people did to him!

Jeremiah: Peace, Baruch. It is God's will. How much money do you need, Hanamel?

Hanamel: Seventeen shekels of silver, cousin.

Jeremiah: Count it out for him, Baruch. It will happen just as the Lord said.

(*He pulls out a small pouch of silver and hands it to Baruch.*)

Baruch: As you wish, master. I also have the deed of purchase ready to sign.

Harim: How could you have known what to write?

Jeremiah: I was ready for you, Harim. The word of the Lord prepared me for this moment.

Baruch: The word of the Lord came to my master and told him that you were coming.

Hanamel: It's amazing! Give me the 17 shekels, and I'll sign. (*Signs the deed.*)

Jeremiah: (*Jeremiah signs the deed and Baruch hands Hanamel a pouch of silver.*) It's done. Go in peace, Hanamel.

Hanamel and Harim: Many thanks, O wise one, many thanks.

Harim (*softly to his father*): I can't believe it! I never thought he would fall for it, Father.

Hanamel: I didn't know what to expect either, my son, but the ways of the Lord are too wonderful for me. (*Hanamel and Harim leave.*)

Crowd (*laughing mockingly*): Hey Jeremiah, I have a swamp for sale. I only need 10 shekels of silver.

Jeremiah: Look here, gentlemen. The Lord God has told me what to do. Baruch, take the documents and put them in a clay jar so that they will last a long time. (*Baruch places the deed in a clay jar.*)

Crowd: I bet there is a cave in Qumran. Store them there— if you can get there.

Baruch: Do you want me to silence them, master?

Jeremiah: Ignore them, Baruch. Listen up, everyone, for this is what the Lord Almighty, the God of Israel, says: "Houses, fields, and vineyards will again be bought in the land."

Zedekiah: What land are you talking about, Jeremiah? I can't figure you out. Will I harvest grapes this year? Is this a positive sign for me?

Jeremiah: Foolish king, I have no more to say to you. Do I have to tell you your fate again? Go now. I must wait for a word from the Lord.

11 – – – ➤ The Fall of Jerusalem

Bible Reference: Jeremiah 39–40:6

Images of cruelty and starvation have become a common part of the news. We have learned to close our eyes and hearts to pictures of toddlers with bloated bellies and staring eyes. It's hard to confront such suffering.

With wrenching grief the writer of Lamentations tells of children who begged their mothers for bread in the streets of Jerusalem. The city withered under the Babylonian siege. The children and infants fainted like wounded men, and their lives ebbed away in their mothers' arms. Judah's stubborn disobedience and unwillingness to submit to God had created this disaster.

Sennacherib's siege ramp at Lachish.

As Jeremiah heard the voices of Babylonian soldiers on the siege ramps outside Jerusalem's walls, he knew that the Babylonians were God's instrument. He also knew that the people of Judah had to submit in order to survive. As he watched the children die and heard stories of horror, Jeremiah agonized over the suffering. Yet he knew that God had begged his children to turn away from danger and disobedience. Because they would not listen, deadly calamity was only hours away.

Some experts suggest that the siege lasted more than two

years. In July 586 B.C. the walls of Jerusalem collapsed under Babylonian battering rams. Babylonian soldiers poured into the city and leveled and buried all of the important buildings, including the temple. Judah would never again be identified as a separate, distinct nation.

In this lesson you will take another look at Zedekiah and Jeremiah. They represent two responses to God's word and two different destinies.

The Lachish Letters

People often save letters that help them recall happy memories. Letters that contain bad news are more often forgotten. In 1935 archaeologists discovered some pieces of pottery near Lachish that tell part of the "bad news" story of Judah's end. Today scholars call the collection of pottery fragments the Lachish Letters.

This ostracon from Gezer possibly contains a list of names.

When the Babylonians invaded Judah they destroyed towns and burned the rubble, crushing any sign of rebellion. By 588 B.C. only three cities of Judah still survived: Azekah, Lachish, and Jerusalem.

A soldier named Hoshaiah was stationed at an outpost north of the city of Lachish. He used the broken pottery pieces to write brief messages to his commander, Yaosh. One of Hoshaiah's tasks was to watch for smoke signals from the city of Azekah and then relay the messages to Yaosh, who was in Lachish.

One day Hoshaiah couldn't see any signals coming from Azekah, and he must have felt frightened and worried about Lachish too. One of the pottery bits, Ostracon Four, ends with, "And let (my lord) know that we are watching for the signals of Lachish, according to all the indications which my lord hath given, for we cannot see Azekah."

Before long Lachish fell to the Babylonians, followed soon after by Jerusalem.

12 ▪ ► Another Deadly Power Struggle

Bible Reference: Jeremiah 40:7—41:15

People often can't agree even when they want to achieve the same thing. Imagine the following scene. Ten students want to play softball at lunch time. They run outside, eager to play; but a disagreement erupts. One group wants to have captains choose teams. The other group wants to number off. Because they can't agree on a method to select teams, they spend most of the recess arguing. They barely begin to play the game when the bell rings. Everyone is irritated as they slowly trail into school.

Adults also indulge in such foolishness, sometimes with disastrous results. Following Jerusalem's destruction the group of people left behind engaged in a power struggle. Everyone wanted the nation of Judah to survive, but they couldn't agree on how to save it. One group wanted to work with the Babylonians. The other group violently opposed Babylonian rule. In this lesson you will see that the result of this conflict was much more serious than a wasted lunch hour. It defined the end of the nation of Judah.

Gedaliah was one of the antagonists. His father, Ahikam, had been an important official in King Josiah's court. Ahikam was one of the messengers that King Josiah sent to consult the prophetess Huldah about the scrolls that they had found in the temple. Following the fall of Jerusalem, Nebuchadnezzar appointed Gedaliah governor, and Jeremiah joined him at Mizpah, the new capital.

Gedaliah's enemy, Ishmael, was of the royal family, which had a history of opposing the Babylonians. Following the fall of Jerusalem he visited King Baalis of Ammon to discuss Judah's future. The Ammonites, distant relatives of the people of Judah, were sometimes known for their lack of hospitality. Maybe Ishmael learned his bad manners from them.

Hospitality

If someone banged on your door in the early hours of the morning, what would you do? Would you offer the person a snack and a place to sleep? Probably not!

If you had lived in Judah during ancient times, you might have grumbled under your breath, but you would have opened the door and said, "Welcome." You would have offered the stranger food and drink and a place to sleep.

A code of hospitality was necessary in a harsh desert land in which you didn't know when you'd need food or shelter. Nearly everyone in the Middle East considered it a sacred duty to offer hospitality to strangers. Some people took the job so seriously that they flew a flag to announce that dinner was ready and guests were welcome.

Guests also followed rules. They were not supposed to take advantage of their hosts; three days was the limit for a visit. A good guest also left a bit of food on his plate to show the host that he had eaten more than enough—a compliment to the host's generosity.

During the early days of the New Testament church, the apostles counted on at least two days of hospitality from sympathetic hosts. This arrangement was good for the apostles and good for their hosts. By entertaining God's messengers, a host became a fellow worker in the spread of the gospel.

We too are called to offer hospitality, but for a new reason. Read Titus 1:8 and 3:1–5a.

13 ------ ➔ Back to Egypt

**Bible Reference: Jeremiah 41:16—44;
Lamentations 3:21–24; Hebrews 10:7–10, 15–18**

Cast: Johanan   Army officer 1
           Azariah, an official   Crowd
           Narrator   Army officer 2
           Jeremiah   Arrogant man

Setting: The public gathering place in the town of Mizpah. The crowd is restless and grumbling.

Johanan: All right, everybody. Listen up! We have plans to make. We don't have much time.

Army officer 1: I say we start out for Egypt tomorrow. I heard that a Babylonian soldier escaped Ishmael's massacre at Mizpah. Nebuchadnezzar will be sending an army to punish us, and it isn't even our fault.

Azariah: I agree. We ought to get out of here as soon as we can.

Crowd: All right! Let's go! We're off to Egypt!

Johanan: Wait just one minute! Why rush into anything? We have at least two weeks before we'll see any of those Babylonians. I think that it makes sense to talk to Jeremiah. He can tell us what God wants us to do.

Azariah: I agree. Let's check with the prophet.

Narrator: So Johanan and all the people—even the old men and babies—went to see Jeremiah.

Johanan: Jeremiah, we know that God's word comes to you, and we really need your advice.

Azariah: We just don't know what to do or where to go.

Army officer 2: Our mission to find and destroy Ishmael was not a total success. We expect incoming Babylonian spears and swords any day now. What is your suggestion, prophet?

Crowd: Yes, pray that the Lord your God will tell us where we should go and what we should do.

Jeremiah: I'll tell you what. I'll pray to the Lord your God and I promise to tell you everything that your God says. I won't hide a thing. Is that really what you want?

Crowd: Yes! Yes! That's what we want.

Johanan: As God is our witness, we'll do everything that you say.

Azariah: We'll do whatever you say, Jeremiah, even if we don't like it.

Army officers: So be it!

Jeremiah: Go then. I'll tell you everything that the Lord says, but you'll have to wait.

Narrator: The people had to wait for ten days before Jeremiah brought them the word of the Lord. Then he called the people together.

Jeremiah: I have a word for you from God: stay.

Crowd: What?

Jeremiah: God wants you to plant and rebuild here in Judah. The Babylonian disaster grieves God, and he wants to restore Judah. Don't go to Egypt. It would be just like going back into slavery.

Arrogant man: Now he tells us.

Johanan: Silence! Let the prophet speak.

Jeremiah: God says to tell you not to be afraid of the king of Babylon. God promises to be with you and to deliver you from the hands of the Babylonians. God promises to have compassion on you.

Army officer 1: It's about time!

Johanan: Is that all God said?

Jeremiah: No, he said more. Are you ready for the rest of the story?

Crowd: Go ahead. Tell it to us.

Jeremiah: Here it is. If you go to Egypt, you will die by the sword, by famine, or by plague.

Johanan: It sounds to me like those curses that Josiah found in Deuteronomy.

Azariah: I think it sounds just like the stories our ancestors told about life in Egypt before the exodus.

Arrogant man: Don't be foolish, Azariah. This situation is entirely different. The Babylonians are our enemy, not the Egyptians.

Jeremiah: I'm not so sure this situation is all that different. You are in serious danger, not from the Babylonians but from the gods and the customs of the Egyptians. Your hearts will be pulled away from God, and once again you will worship the things your hands have made instead of the Creator God.

Crowd (grumbling and mumbling): What good has God done us lately? The Egyptian gods couldn't possibly do any worse.

Jeremiah: You asked me to tell you everything that God said, and you said that you would obey. Now listen well and understand. Going to Egypt will be a fatal mistake. If you go to Egypt, you will surely die. The place you thought would give you peace and safety will destroy you.

Johanan: You are lying! The Lord would never tell you to say that!

Arrogant man: Surely your servant Baruch has put you up to this. He'd like to see us punished by the Babylonians for all of your suffering.

Jeremiah: Don't be foolish. Trust God, and stay in Judah.

Johanan (turning to the people): What shall we do? Shall we stay here as the prophet commanded?

Crowd: No! No!

Johanan: Shall we go to Egypt?

Crowd: To Egypt! To Egypt!

Narrator: So Johanan and all the people disobeyed the word of the Lord to stay in Judah. Instead, all of the men, women, children, and king's daughters entered Egypt in disobedience to the Lord. And Jeremiah and Baruch went with them.

Unit 7
Days of Exile

1 – – – – → A Vision and a Call

Bible Reference: Ezekiel 1–3, 18, 33

What would you think if at church one Sunday, when it was time for the sermon, your pastor stretched out on the floor in front of the congregation and didn't say a word? Can you imagine what it would be like if your pastor "preached" this same sermon for a year of Sundays?

The Bible says that the prophet Ezekiel spent 390 days on his left side and then 40 more days on his right side. Ezekiel "spoke" with actions that we might consider odd, and he created powerful pictures, sometimes without words.

But Ezekiel's words and actions were not particularly strange to the exiles in Babylon. For hundreds of years, in worship gatherings and around campfires, the people of God had been telling stories of fiery chariots, of miraculous healings, and even of resurrections. When Ezekiel preached by showing, the people understood. They knew that Ezekiel's long days stretched out on the ground represented their long unavoidable days of exile.

This preaching episode was not the only dramatic episode in Ezekiel's career. In this lesson you will read about Ezekiel's vision and his call from God. His vision was

Ezekiel Prophesying by Gustave Doré.

fantastic, so majestic and strange that Ezekiel was overwhelmed and fell flat on his face. In his vision he saw God's glory. God's presence was filled with such brilliance and splendor that Ezekiel couldn't stand it.

Ezekiel, a young man from a priestly family, was taken to Babylon with the first wave of exiles in 597 B.C., about ten years before the fall of Jerusalem. His style was more dramatic, but the heart of his message was the same as Jeremiah's. They both proclaimed and explained God's judgment on the people of Judah.

During the first few years in Babylon, many of the exiles hoped for a quick return to their homeland. But for six years Ezekiel vividly told them that this would not happen; Jerusalem would fall. And it did. After the fall of Jerusalem, Ezekiel's message changed to one of hope. Like the prophets before him, Ezekiel offered God's promise of restoration and healing.

Smile

Have you ever been really down and wanted to be alone and then one of your parents said, "Why the long face? C'mon, smile!" You felt like crying, but you turned angrily away before the tears could show.

Something like that happened to the people in exile in Babylon. They could hardly bear it when the people mockingly asked them to sing the songs of Jerusalem. Here is their reaction.

A minstrel with his harp.

> By the rivers of Babylon we sat and wept
>   when we remembered Zion.
> There on the poplars
>   we hung our harps,
> for there our captors asked us for songs,
>   our tormentors demanded songs of joy;
>   they said, "Sing us one of the songs of Zion!"
> How can we sing the songs of the Lord
>   while in a foreign land?
>
> Psalm 137:1–4

2 - - - ➤ Scattering Hair in the Wind

Bible Reference: Ezekiel 4–5

There are some gestures that nearly everyone understands. Most people know that you are communicating "yes" when you nod your head up and down. When you extend your hand with the palm facing outward, it usually means stay away. Can you think of other commonly-understood gestures? Are some gestures specific to your part of the world?

To get his point across, Ezekiel created a variety of images. He used dramatic mime and familiar gestures to warn about the judgment the Babylonians were going to inflict on Jerusalem.

Sometimes Ezekiel's symbolic acts are difficult to understand, especially because they occurred over 2,000 years ago. As you read about Ezekiel's messages, remember that prophets represented God's presence among the people of Israel and Judah. If the people rejected the prophets, they symbolically rejected God. If a prophet was separated from the people, it was a symbol that God was no longer with the people.

Knowing about peasant food will also help you understand Ezekiel's message. Peasants ate mainly grains, not meat. Their bread was not made with finely ground wheat but with barley and other grains. Why would Jerusalem be reduced to eating peasant food and rationing water?

Now about hair. For some people baldness symbolized public shame. For Isaiah it was a sign of repentance, and for Micah it was a sign of mourning. It was not a desirable condition. Yet God instructed Ezekiel to shave his head and his beard. As you read the story of the hair blowing in the wind, look for ways that Ezekiel's message resembles the message of other prophets.

God put Ezekiel on a meager diet of limited bread and water to represent Judah's coming starvation. Ezekiel's scant water supply was measured in baths. In Ezekiel's time the word *bath* didn't have anything to do with a steaming tub of hot water. A bath was a unit of liquid measure that equaled about 38.5 pints or 22 liters. In Ezekiel 4 God instructed Ezekiel to drink one sixth of a hin of water. A hin equaled one sixth of a bath. How much water did Ezekiel drink each day?

3 ----→ The Glory Departs

Bible Reference: Ezekiel 8–11

What do you think three-year-olds or four-year-olds would say if you asked them where God lives? They might say that God lives all around us, that God lives in our hearts, or even that God lives in church.

In Ezekiel's time both children and adults would have said that God lived in the temple. They grew up hearing stories of God's presence leading the people with an awesome pillar of fire. Everyone also knew that after Solomon built the temple, God moved in.

The temple, which represented God's presence with the people, gave them security and a center of worship. In order for God to dwell with his people, however, they had to be "fully committed to the Lord our God, to live by his decrees and obey his commands" (1 Kings 8:61).

By Ezekiel's time it was clear that the people were not fully committed to God. Their pagan practices polluted their worship. The people tried to insure good crops and healthy herds by worshiping Canaanite fertility gods as well as God. In this lesson you will read about some temple activities that

A *taw*, the last letter of the Hebrew alphabet, was the mark put on the foreheads of the people in Jerusalem who grieved and lamented over all of the wicked things that were being done there (Ezekiel 9:4).

The Five Abominations

God gave Ezekiel a vision of five terrible things that happened at the temple. The following glossary explains the abominations found in Ezekiel 8 and the resulting judgment described in Ezekiel 9.

The idol of jealousy—a statue of Asherah, a Canaanite fertility goddess.

Animal portraits on the temple walls—Egyptian religious influence.

Tammuz—a Babylonian fertility god who supposedly caused plants to wilt when he died.

Bowing to the sun with backs to the temple—worship of one of Egypt's main gods, the sun god Re.

Putting the branch to their nose—a ceremonial gesture connected to violence in Ezekiel 8:17.

On this section of the Book of the Dead (1300 B.C.) the sun god Re is shown with a falcon head.

were anything but holy. God gave Ezekiel a vision of the action in the temple and the killing of the idolaters. And then something terrible and solemn happened: God's glory left the temple. The peoples' wickedness drove God's presence from the temple.

4 ‒ ‒ ‒ ‒ ‒ ➤ The Glory Returns

> **Bible Reference: Ezekiel 11:17–23; 43:1–11; 47:1–12; selected New Testament passages**

How do you feel when you step out of the shower after a sweaty game of basketball or a day of dirty work? That feeling of being totally clean is just a taste of what it will feel like to swim in the river that flows from the throne of God.

The people living in exile in Babylon must have felt dirty and ashamed when they listened to all of Ezekiel's prophecies of doom. They had heard some of Jeremiah's sermons, so when Ezekiel described his vision of a crystal clear river, the people must have imagined what it would be like to dive into that river. To lounge on its banks and eat the fruit ripe for picking all year long must have seemed like a dream. The best part of the vision was that God's glory had returned to the temple and brought with it a healing river that gushed out of the temple.

For God's presence to return, the temple needed to be cleansed and the people needed to turn their hearts to God. God promised to give the people new hearts. God was getting ready to do some heart cleaning.

Jesus, the Messiah, made it possible for God's people to make their hearts a good place for God to live. The Messiah has come. But just as the exiles in Babylon longed to go home, we are waiting for Jesus to come again and make all things clean and new. Some day we will walk with God in the New Jerusalem.

5 ▬ ▬ ▬ ▬ ➤ The Good Shepherd

Bible Reference: Ezekiel 34; John 10:1–18

Before the exile, the people's lives back in Judah had been quite simple. Even Judah's leaders understood the demands and the routine of tending sheep. Most of the exiles were probably familiar with Jacob's deathbed confession that God had been his shepherd all his life (Genesis 48:15), and they may have even memorized Psalm 23 as children.

In this lesson we are going to listen to Ezekiel's straightforward shepherd sermon. Ezekiel's parting words in this sermon point us ahead to one of Jesus' most beautiful sermons, the New Testament story of the good shepherd. Through Ezekiel God said, "You are my sheep, and I am your God." Jesus said, "I am the good shepherd; I know my sheep and my sheep know me—and I lay down my life for the sheep."

Shepherds were quite important in Old Testament times. Shepherds were like bankers, because sheep represented wealth. A single sheep was very valuable, and the loss of one meant disaster for a poor family. For even the wealthy the loss of one sheep meant the loss of a significant amount of wool, milk, and meat.

A Bedouin shepherd with his sheep.

The person who tended the sheep was responsible for the investments of a family or sometimes of the whole community.

To succeed, shepherds had to protect the sheep. Shepherds used slings and clubs to protect the sheep from lions and other beasts. When they were far from home, they built protective stone walls to keep the sheep safe. They used their staffs to rescue stray sheep from crevasses and to prod reluctant sheep back onto the path.

But shepherds needed more than weapons to succeed. The really good shepherds knew all of their sheep by name. When a good shepherd called, the sheep all recognized his voice and immediately followed. If several herds were mixed together at a watering hole, all a shepherd needed to do was to give his distinctive call, and the sheep would sort themselves from the others to follow him.

Because they knew that their shepherd would protect and feed them, sheep trusted and followed him. Good shepherds did not need to drive their sheep from behind. The sheep knew their shepherd's voice and followed without being forced.

What image do you think that Jesus would use today to help us understand his incredible love for us? Would he say, "I am the good orchestra conductor" or "the good drama director"? What about, "I am the good coach?" It doesn't matter whether we are called sheep, musicians, or volleyball players. We are all precious to the Good Shepherd, and he wants to bring us all into the flock.

6 — — — ➤ The Valley of Dry Bones

Bible Reference: Ezekiel 37

Narrator: It was 11 P.M. on a Friday night, and Jon wished that he was in bed. Tomorrow was going to be one of the busiest days of his life. He had to play bassoon in the regional music festival in the morning, the coach had scheduled an extra basketball practice for the afternoon, and there was going to be a class party at night. Unfortunately, before his parents would allow him to participate in any extracurricular activities, they always checked to make sure that all of his assignments were finished— and not just plain ordinary finished but finished flawlessly. Jon groaned as he looked at his Bible assignments and wished aloud for Ezekiel to come and help him. And then he heard a voice.

Ezekiel: You seem to be a bit sur . . . uh . . . unhappy.

Jon: Go ahead and say it. I'm surly. You'd be surly too if your parents made you do your homework on a Friday night. I know the weekend will be busy, but do you know anyone else in the world who does homework on Friday night?

Ezekiel: No, but then I don't know anyone else in the world at the moment.

Jon: What makes you think you know me?

Ezekiel: Let's find out. Is it true that you were just groaning over your Bible assignment?

Jon: Yes, but so what?

Ezekiel: Patience. Is your assignment from the Book of Ezekiel?

Jon: Yes, but . . .

Ezekiel (interrupting): OK then, I'm your man. See, I do know something about you. My name is Ezekiel. (*Reaches out to shake Jon's hand.*) Pleased to meet you, Jon. Your name is Jon, isn't it?

Jon: Yes. I'm pleased to meet you too. And, um . . . I'm not this surly all the time, really. Actually your book is pretty interesting and uh . . . bizarre all at the same time—no offense. The first chapter— you know, the one about the wheels and the eyes—is like something out of *Star Wars*.

Ezekiel: No offense taken. But why do you people fight with stars? By the way, don't worry about having trouble understanding my writing. People have always said that my book was difficult to understand. So now's your chance to ask me anything you want about the book. I'll explain everything I can, but a lot has happened since I was last on earth.

Jon: One thing that I'd like to know is why did you always describe stuff in such weird ways. Why didn't you just come out and say what you were thinking.

Ezekiel: Think about this, Jon. Isn't it easier for you to remember an idea if you can connect it with a picture? I didn't want the people to tune me out. So I acted out some scenes, and God gave me incredible visions to explain what had happened and what would happen. Don't people today keep pictures in their heads to help them remember things?

Jon: I guess we do, but I think we keep more of them in our computers—but we're not going to talk about computers, are we?

Ezekiel: There's one more thing about my writing that you should know. Sometimes I use words that have several meanings, and the meanings work together all at the same time. Like the word *blue*, for example. It can mean the color of the sky or it can mean feeling anxious, worried, or depressed. So the color blue in a painting or in a poem can mean sadness and depression.

Jon: OK, I get your point. I don't want to be rude or anything, but can we get to the assignment?

Ezekiel: Of course. What part of my book are you studying?

Jon: I have to do something with the story of the bones. Do you know the song about dried up old bones hearing the word of the Lord and dancing with life?

Ezekiel: I don't think that I know the song, but I do know the story. It was one of the most exciting visions that God gave me.

Jon: I don't understand it.

Ezekiel: I think that you know more about the story than you realize, Jon. Do you remember how Isaiah used the vineyard to symbolize the people of God? All of the prophets used words and images to represent other ideas and events. If you can find some symbols in this story, maybe it

The Vision of Ezekiel by Gustave Doré.

will make more sense. I'll give you some clues, and you see if you can guess the meaning.

Jon: OK, let's get going.

Ezekiel: Let's start with the first verses. If you walked through a field filled with bones, what would your first question be?

Jon: I dunno. I suppose I'd ask who died there.

Ezekiel: Now think. Who might the bones represent?

Jon: Some dead people?

Ezekiel: Of course, the bones could represent dead people. But who had been slaughtered at Jerusalem, and who was my audience?

Jon: I think I get it. The bones stand for the people of Judah who had been killed by the Babylonians. Right?

Ezekiel: You're on the right track. Let's push the symbol of bones just a bit further.

Jon: All right.

Ezekiel: Take the word *dead*, for example. After running a marathon, a woman dropping from exhaustion might say, "I'm dead!" Clearly she's not dead, but she is very tired. Here's another example. What would your older brother say if he got pulled over by a police officer because he was speeding?

Jon: He'd say, "I'm dead." By the way, how did you know he's about to lose his driver's license?

Ezekiel: Don't ask. I think you almost have it. How would we describe someone without energy, without ambition, and without hope or joy?

Jon: We'd say they're dead. Oh, now I see. The people of Judah living in

Babylon didn't have any hope for the future because they thought that God had abandoned them. Say, Ezekiel, do you know about the New Testament and about the apostle Paul? He used the word *dead* in another way. He said that some people are dead in sin but are made alive in Christ. Would you like to hear about Paul?

Ezekiel: I would. But before we start on this Paul person, can you tell me what God was saying to the people in Babylon by putting the skeletons back together?

Jon: No problem. He was telling them to have hope in spite of the terrible stuff the Babylonians had done to them.

Ezekiel: Now you're thinking symbolically! When you read the rest of the passage, watch carefully for the promises connected with the connected bones. Now, let's start on the word *breath*. Here's your clue. What's the earliest reference in the Bible to the breath of God? Can you get this part on your own?

Jon: I think so, but will you be around to help me?

Ezekiel: You really don't need me anymore, Jon. So long. And by the way, I hope you don't feel dead after your long day tomorrow.

7 ▬ ▬ ▬ ▬ ▬ ➤ Keeping the Faith

Bible Reference: Daniel 1–6

Did you ever have to move away from your friends, school, and church because your mom or dad took a new job in a different place? Perhaps you were sure that you'd "just die" without your best friend, and you did everything you could think of to make your parents feel guilty. Then as you slowly got used to your new home, you forgot about your old one. Another best friend entered the scene, and you stopped plotting ways to go back.

The days of exile in Babylon created similar stresses for the people of Judah. At first they felt disoriented and horribly discouraged. God seemed

Once the Jewish exiles got a grip on life in Babylon and were able to look around without weeping, they discovered an amazing city. Towering arches decorated with bold, blue-glazed tile graced the massive walls surrounding Babylon. The walls were strong and wide enough for two chariots to ride next to each other on the top.

The exiles discovered other evidence of Babylonian resourcefulness. Ingenious air vents in Babylonian homes let in cool breezes but kept out the rats. And Babylonian swimmers crossed the Euphrates River with the help of crude life preservers—inflated goat skins. These goat skins also provided buoyancy for heavily loaded cargo rafts. Elaborate irrigation systems watered fruit trees that yielded succulent fruits: apricots, plums, peaches, figs, and pomegranates. Thanks to Babylonian farming skills, the savory aroma of leeks simmering with mint and garlic floated through open windows at dinnertime. Babylon wasn't a bad place to live.

Daniel and his friends were probably taught to read and write cuneiform in one of the schools for scribes. Because of this training, they were able to read many of the myths associated with Babylonian gods. Archaeologists discovered many of these Babylonian myths when they unearthed the great Assyrian library collection by Assurbanipal at Nineveh. They excavated almost 30,000 clay tablets that hold works of religion, science, and mathematics from that site.

The Babylonians used a system of numbering by sixties that mathematicians still use today. Our concept of time as seconds, minutes, and hours is based on this Babylonian numbering system. We also owe our understanding of circles to this system of sixties, because we divide circles into 360 degrees.

It's no wonder that the exiles were tempted to stay in Babylon. It was one of the great attractions of the ancient world.

Assurbanipal was the last great king of Assyria. During his reign Assyria became the leading world power.

to have abandoned them; after all, he hadn't protected them from the Babylonian destroyers. They had no hope and little joy.

But life in Babylon eventually proved to be fairly agreeable for the exiles. They were permitted to build houses and to live together in settlements. Babylon was one of the great centers of world culture. In contrast, Jerusalem must have seemed a poor and backward place. It must have been tempting for the exiles to throw away their customs—and even their faith—in their new surroundings.

Daniel was deported in the first group of exiles during Jehoiakim's reign in 605 B.C., so Daniel was in Babylon at the same time as Ezekiel. Daniel came from a noble family. He was young, talented, and handsome. That's why he was one of the youths selected to receive special training for three years at the king's court. After this training, he would enter the king's service.

It took great courage and strong faith for Daniel to live in the king's court and still hold on to the beliefs and customs of his own people. And through the stories of their obedience, Daniel and his three friends have become role models of courage and faith to others persecuted for their faith.

But the Book of Daniel also emphasizes something else. Daniel wanted to show that God is and always will be victorious. In story after story God wins. These stories show that God is faithful and powerful in helping his people and that God is sovereign (supreme, in control of all things). Keep this emphasis in mind as you read the stories from the Book of Daniel.

Daniel by Michelangelo from the Sistine Chapel, painted 1508–1512.

8 ━ ━ ━ ━ ➤ Four Beasts and the Ancient of Days

Bible Reference: Daniel 7

A deafening shriek, thundering sound effects, and flashing darkness announced Aslan's death and caused angry tears at a recent dramatic production of *The Lion, the Witch, and the Wardrobe.* Before long Aslan's resurrection and his promise of final victory brought cheers of joy from the audience of elementary school students. In spite of all the horrors that the white witch had inflicted on Narnia, the lion could not be ultimately defeated. The children applauded as Aslan took his curtain call, and many left the theater eager to read the other Narnia tales, written by C.S. Lewis shortly after World War II ended. In his books Lewis acknowledges that sin and evil have invaded our world, but God and good always win.

Apocalyptic literature is something like the Narnia tales. In fantastic visions, terrifying clashes between the forces of good and evil end in the ultimate triumph of God over sin's power. Daniel 7 contains several visions of future events, complete with four hideous beasts and the white-haired

The Work of the Beast

Daniel's vision of the terrifying beast pointed ahead to a time of persecution for God's people during the days of the Roman Empire. Many early Christians, such as Polycarp, willingly faced death rather than deny their loyalty to Jesus.

Polycarp grew up in the church of the apostle John and later became the beloved bishop of Smyrna. Smyrna was a thriving port on the Aegean Sea during the Roman era. It is now the Turkish city of Izmir.

At the time of his death in 156 A.D. Polycarp was an old man. When faced with renouncing Jesus or being burned at the stake, Polycarp said, "Eighty and six years have I served him, and he has never done me wrong; how can I blaspheme him, my King, who has saved me? I am a Christian."

The Dragon Wants to Devour the Infant by Giusto Giovanni Mendabuoi, 1363.

Ancient of Days sitting on a throne of fire. Before you look closely at Daniel's vision, let's look as some of the main features of apocalyptic literature.

- It divides the universe into two camps: good and evil.
- It focuses on the future and presents a scenario of final events.
- It is full of visions and symbols. The deep and mysterious things the prophet is trying to communicate are told in extraordinary language.
- It pictures a time of difficulty and tribulation for God's people followed by a great triumph for God and his people.
- It comforts and encourages God's people with the vision of God's ultimate triumph over evil.

In this lesson you will be looking carefully at apocalyptic passages in the Book of Daniel and in the Book of Revelation. You will find God's reassuring promise that the destruction of evil will surely come. The early Christians knew what it was like to live in terrible times. Do you ever wonder how our times compare with those times?

9 ━ ━ ━ ➤ For Such a Time as This

Bible Reference: The Book of Esther

Haman, the king's right hand man, was a bully. He did not fear God, and he hated God's people, the Jews. Haman had descended from the God-hating Amalekites, and he carried on their tradition of hostility to God. He especially hated Mordecai, the Jew who refused to show him respect. Mordecai, on the other hand, cared deeply about the safety and long-term survival of the Jewish people. He acted in belief that life is guided by God's hand. These antagonists, Haman and Mordecai, represent the conflict between good and evil, between the belief that life just happens and the belief that God guides life.

The setting for the Book of Esther is the time of the Jewish exile in Susa, the Persian capital city. By this time Persia was the major world power, and Xerxes was the Persian king. Xerxes, who reigned from 486–465 B.C., lacked the wisdom and good judgment of his father, Darius. Around 480 B.C. he picked a fight with the Greeks and was soundly defeated. After that, Xerxes spent his time restoring temples and entertaining himself with a lavish lifestyle.

As you read the story of Esther, watch for the feasts and the fasts. You

Persepolis was another capital city during the reigns of Darius and Xerxes.

will see how the feasts start out as drunken self-indulgent revels, turn into places of revelation and judgment, and then become a joyful celebration of God's goodness. The fasts are also significant. The prophet Amos would probably have been pleased with Esther's fast because she did not intend it as a performance to win God's favor. It was an admission of human weakness and need. As a community the Jewish people looked to God for guidance during a frightening crisis.

The Book of Esther also speaks to us about the conflict of loyalties that both Esther and Mordecai experienced. They both had reasons to be loyal to the king. They had actually combined their efforts to save King Xerxes from assassins. But their loyalty to God's chosen people was greater. A highlight of the story of Esther is her courageous decision to be loyal to God and to the Jewish people. Facing down Haman was dangerous, but God fulfilled his side of the covenant.

Purim

After defeating Haman, Esther and Mordecai were unstoppable. Together they began a feast that Jews still celebrate today. It is the Jewish festival called Purim. It gets its name from *pur*, the word for the object the Persians used to cast lots. Haman believed that our lives are determined by fate, the "roll of the dice." When he cast lots to determine the day to exterminate the Jews, the lot fell on the twelfth month, Adar. To this day, Jewish people celebrate Purim in February or March, the time that corresponds to the month of Adar.

To celebrate their deliverance from the evil Haman, many Jewish people give gifts to each other and to the poor. They also eat three-cornered, fruit-filled pastries called hamantaschen that remind them of Haman's hat. The most important part of the Purim celebration is the retelling of the story of Esther. For some, the reading of the story is a playful, joyous event. Whenever the storyteller mentions Haman's name, the people jeer, stamp their feet, and create a ruckus with noisemakers called graggers.

1 ━ ━ ━ ━ ━ ➤ Back to Jerusalem

Bible Reference: Ezra 1–3

Have you ever helped plan a family vacation or dreamed about a special weekend away from home? If you have, you probably understand the saying "Getting there is half the fun." Sometimes when the anticipation is great the actual event is a little disappointing.

For the people in Babylon, talk of returning to Jerusalem inspired memories of a grand and beautiful temple. The old folks told stories of the glory days of David and Solomon. In 539 B.C. Cyrus issued a decree that allowed

A Real Nest Egg

Before the exiles set out on their adventure to Jerusalem, God worked in the hearts of the Persian leaders and in the hearts of the Jews who chose to stay behind. They gave generously to support the rebuilding of the temple. The supporters gave priestly garments, 61,000 drachmas of gold, and 5,000 minas of silver.

Some experts believe that the drachma mentioned in Ezra 2:69 might be a gold Persian coin called a daric. The Persian ruler Darius drew attention to his power and authority by minting the daric. It shows him holding a scepter and a bow. This coin may have appeared in Babylon around 500 B.C.

According to the Mesopotamian number system, there were 50 shekels in a mina and 60 minas in a talent. One shekel (about two-fifths of an ounce of silver) equaled the pay an average person might receive for one month of work. How many years would an average person have to work to earn one mina?

Can you figure out how many talents of silver the exiles took back to Jerusalem?

Stone weights used to measure money.

This barrel is like the one that Cyrus inscribed allowing the Jews to return to Jerusalem.

the Jews to return home. Some responded with joy and immediately began to plan their return trip. Anticipating their return to Judah was exciting. Even the Jews who decided to stay in Babylon helped pay for the trip.

The leaders of the first group to return were Zerubbabel and Sheshbazzar. They were descendants of David and were closely related to Judah's last Davidic king, Jehoiachin. The group's journey proved to be difficult and dangerous. Their nest egg of gold and silver was probably a temptation for highway robbers. But God was with them and brought them safely through. When they reached Jerusalem, their enthusiasm led them to make immediate building plans. What do you think they chose to rebuild first, the protecting walls of the city or a temple for God?

2 ■ ➤ Skirmishes with the Samaritans

Bible Reference: Ezra 4–6:12

The Samaritan settlers who were living in Jewish territory probably wished that the Jews had never left Babylon. They were worried about Jewish plans for Jerusalem and saw the return of the exiles as a threat to their interests in the region. They used all sorts of tricks to get the exiles in trouble with the Persian rulers. Were they tattletales?

The Samaritans were not the only obstacle the Jewish exiles faced. Food was scarce because crops failed several times in the early years after the return. So the Jews also faced hunger and even starvation.

Their early struggles highlighted the need for unified answers to some pretty basic questions: Who are we and what are we doing here? Why did we come back to Judah? Should we rebuild the temple first, or should we worry about safety and rebuild the walls of the city? Whom should we trust?

The Samaritan ritual bath at Mount Gerizim.

The Jewish exiles did not agree on the answers to these questions. Some were committed to rebuilding the temple. Some cared more about establishing a national identity. Others thought it was foolish to worry about the temple when they were faced with failing crops and hungry children.

In this lesson the stories of opposition to the Jews occur in the context of four Persian kings: Cyrus, Darius I, Xerxes, and Artaxerxes. These stories

Persian Spies

It must have annoyed the Jews to always have the Samaritans snooping around looking for ways to make trouble. But if the Samaritans hadn't spied on them, someone else would have. The Persian kings had elaborate spy systems. Two government officials were actually called the King's Eye and the King's Ear. They reported everything they saw and heard to the king. Military  spies informed on government employees, and government spies kept an eye on military leaders. Their regular reports to the king made it possible for him to stamp out rebellion before it could really get started.

Early in the reign of Darius I there was unrest and revolt in the Persian empire. Some scholars think that Persian spies heard about patriots in Judah who wanted to make Zerubbabel king. Historians do not know what happened to Zerubbabel. We do know that his name disappeared from historical records around this time. Maybe he was removed because he challenged Persian authority. Maybe the people of Judah needed to find their glory and strength in their identity as God's children.

What was Jesus' attitude toward Samaritans? John 4:39–42 gives us an idea.

Many of the Samaritans from Sychar believed in Jesus because of the woman's testimony—"He told me everything I ever did." So when the Samaritans came to Jesus, they urged him to stay with them, and he stayed two days. And because of his words many more became believers.

They said to the woman, "We no longer believe just because of what you said; now we have heard for ourselves, and we know that this man really is the Savior of the world."

Jesus' words changed hostile Samaritans into believers and brought them into his kingdom.

Jesus probably spoke with the Samaritan woman at a well like this.

cover a timespan of more than 50 years, from 538 B.C. to sometime before 445 B.C. They show God's faithfulness in protecting his people and preserving a remnant to fulfill his purposes. If kings cannot block God's plan, tattletales don't have a chance.

3 ━ ━ ━ ➤ The Heart of the Temple

Bible Reference: Haggai 1–2:9

Human beings have the ability to create beauty to solve problems. We also have the ability to sidestep responsibility. At an early age most of us learn to blame others for our sins. "It's his fault" or "She made me do it" are excuses as old as Eden. When the prophet Haggai asked why the temple was still in ruins, the people may have said, "It's the Samaritans' fault. They wouldn't let us work."

The people had been back in Judah for around 18 years, and the temple still sat in ruins. Soon after their return to Jerusalem the people had begun to rebuild the foundation. After that they did little more. Instead, they focused on rebuilding their farms and scrambling to raise money for taxes. They did not take time to come together to worship and

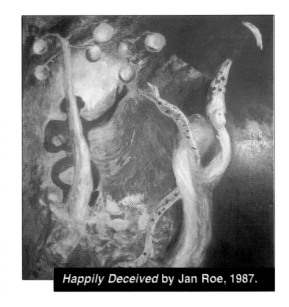

Happily Deceived by Jan Roe, 1987.

praise God. As they became less centered on God, they became more self-centered and dishonest. It seemed that the old sin of oppressing the poor was creeping back into Judah. Judah's conscience was sleeping. In 520 B.C. Haggai decided to wake them up.

Like a blast of cold air his pointed sermons woke them up. With sharp questions Haggai made it clear that Judah's neglect of the temple was causing their troubles. Haggai's enthusiasm for rebuilding the temple grew out of deep beliefs. He was convinced that the temple represented God's plan

A First Rate Postal System

Who said it? "Neither snow nor rain nor heat nor gloom of night stays these couriers from the swift completion of their appointed rounds." If you guessed that Benjamin Franklin said it, you are wrong. An ancient historian named Herodotus gave the Persian postal system high marks with these words.

In the third century the Persian pony express was able to move a piece of mail over 100 miles a day. Persian letter carriers relied on a network of well-designed highways. We often credit the Romans and their roads for the spread of the gospel. But the Persians probably taught the Romans a thing or two about road construction and about postal systems.

and promises. Haggai pointed to a time when God would construct his temple using believers made alive through Christ—living stones.

Like the other prophets, Haggai was an important builder of God's kingdom. But the Bible doesn't tell us much about him. He may have seen Solomon's temple before it was destroyed by the Babylonians. If that is the case, Haggai must have been around 70 years old when he began preaching. The Book of Haggai is short, and Haggai's ministry lasted only four months. Yet his effective preaching showed that like all true prophets Haggai was another genuine voice of God. The people of Judah were convinced. They stopped whining and started to work.

4 — — ➤ Zechariah, a Man of Vision

Bible Reference: Zechariah 1–6

Have you ever heard your pastor solemnly say, "And God spake all these words saying"? Not many ministers still read the Ten Commandments with the same somber tone as they did long ago. Some don't read the commandments more than four or five times a year. And almost no one reads them in King James English.

The language of some of the commandments was not always easy to understand. One phrase in the fourth commandment was particularly confusing. Exodus 20:5 says, "I, the Lord your God, am a jealous God."

It seems strange to say that God is jealous. But God's jealousy is different from human jealousy. God's emotions do not contain the self-centered anger that afflicts us when we don't get the attention we think we deserve. God's jealousy is more like the heartbroken anger of a deserted husband or wife. Because God longs to have us back where we belong, he found a way to bring us home. Jesus paid the price of our unfaithfulness.

In the Book of Zechariah you will find eight vivid visions that paint a picture of God. With images of a loving, powerful, and jealous God,

Have you ever seen someone get so angry that his or her face became beet red? The Hebrew word for jealousy is *qin' ˆå*. Some scholars think that its meaning came from an Arabic word that means "to become intensely red with dye." The word probably refers to the color produced when we experience deep emotion and blood floods our faces.

The English word for jealousy comes from the Greek word *zeo*. It means "to boil." Our jealousy is often a self-centered scalding thing that destroys relationships and ruins friendships.

But God's jealousy is different. It brought about the greatest restoration and healing in the history of humankind. Like the prophets before him, Zechariah knew that God's jealousy would produce the messiah.

Zechariah encouraged the people to rebuild the temple. Like Haggai, Zechariah wanted the people to put God at the center of their lives. As you read Zechariah's visions, think about our God. He loves his people as much today as in 420 B.C. when Zechariah and Haggai were the preachers. Even if you don't hear the Ten Commandments every Sunday, keep listening for the jealous love of God.

5 – – – – ➤ The Coming Messiah

**Bible Reference: Selected passages from
Zechariah 9–14**

Can you imagine what it would be like to play on a basketball team that didn't win a single game in three years? Can you imagine what it would be like to be the coach! The exiles had experienced more than 15 losing seasons, and they were ready to give up their dream of a new temple. They had muddled along without a coach until Haggai delivered his halftime sermon. Zechariah joined the team shortly after Haggai. Together the two prophets whipped up enthusiasm for the temple project. And the people built the new temple within four years.

Zechariah's name meant "The Lord Remembers." Zechariah reminded the people that God had not forgotten his covenant promises. One of those promises was that a messiah would come.

The gospel writers of the New Testament knew that Zechariah's promises of hope reached all the way to them. They often quoted Zechariah when they told the story of Jesus.

Jesus is the messiah that Zechariah told about. And wherever Jesus is Lord, wherever people serve him and live for him, God's kingdom comes. Yet we are waiting for these things to be true everywhere and all of the time. And this will not happen until Jesus comes again.

The Lord began a huge project when he decided to turn a bunch of losers into winners. The changes have begun. But we have to wait for his second coming to have a perfect season.

6 – – – ➔ Ezra Tears His Hair Out

> **Bible Reference: Ezra 7–10**

Haggai and Zechariah's mission to get the temple rebuilt was successful. Many years after the temple was completed in 516 B.C. a famous Jewish priest named Ezra lived in Babylon and was active in the king's court. A descendent of Aaron, he devoted himself to studying and teaching the law of God. Around 458 B.C. God worked in the heart of Ezra and encouraged him to return to Jerusalem. It seems that Ezra was just the man to tackle a problem simmering in there.

Let's listen in on one of Ezra's conversations.

Michael: Say, Ezra, have you heard the news? The Persians aren't the only ones with eyes and ears. Artaxerxes has said yes!

Ezra: Wait a minute. Let me finish writing down this last commandment. These old manuscripts are so fragile. I want to make sure that we have a good copy of God's law when we go back to Jerusalem.

Michael: That's just it, Ezra. I have news about the Jerusalem expedition. My cousin Joel says that Artaxerxes' scribe is already writing out the royal decree. In just a few days we will have his official permission to go home. And I hear that he is giving us even more than we asked for.

Ezra: How would you know? Did you have lunch with the king?

Michael: Didn't I tell you that the Persians aren't the only ones with special eyes and ears? Joel's son, Nathan, was given the task of sweeping the royal floor. The king's advisors discuss all sorts of things in front of him. They must think that he doesn't have ears.

Ezra: It's quite clear that you have ears—and a mouth too. What did he say?

Michael: Listen, that must be Nathan coming now. Let him tell you. (*Nathan runs in.*) Nathan, where have you been? I told you to hurry! Tell Ezra what you heard.

Ezra: Take your time, Nathan. We're eager to leave Babylon, but you have time to breathe. Would you like something to drink?

Nathan: No, master. I'm all right. My cousin is a little impatient. Aren't you eager to hear my story too?

Ezra: Yes, I am. Sit down and tell us.

Nathan: Well, the king's advisors aren't very happy, but what can they do? The king has spoken. Any Israelite who wishes to go back to Jerusalem with you may go. The advisors are complaining that the king is going to give you a whole lot of silver and gold. They say that he will even give you some golden vessels for the temple.

Michael (*sourly*): Why should that bother them? They were our temple vessels to begin with.

Nathan: I don't think the advisors really care about the temple stuff. They're more worried about what the treasurers back in Palestine will say. The king's letter says that the Samaritans had better not tax us when we get back to Judah. And they have to give us all the silver, wheat, wine, and olive oil that we need.

Michael: It's about time! Letters from my relatives in Jerusalem say that life has been pretty rough. God's people deserve a break.

Ezra: I'm not sure that we deserve a break, Michael. If your relatives' letters are correct, there's something wrong in the city of Jerusalem. It might be better if we don't get what we deserve. Do you have anything else to report, Nathan?

Nathan: Yes, sir. Just one more thing. The king trusts you because he thinks that there's something different about you. He says that God's hand is on you. That's good, right?

Ezra: I'd say, yes. It's good. The king thinks that our God's laws are the best around. But let's talk more about the law some other time. We have plans to complete. Michael, will you . . .

Michael (interrupting): Shall I ask for a military escort, Ezra?

Ezra: Whatever for?

Michael: Don't think for one minute that the desert bandits haven't heard rumors about our gifts from the king. They'll skin us alive before we are 100 miles from Babylon.

Ezra: Michael, Michael. We don't need an armed escort. God's gracious hand is on everyone who looks to him.

Michael: Have it your way. What was it you wanted me to do?

7 − − ➤ Nehemiah, a Master Builder

Bible Reference: Nehemiah 1–6

You can see heart shapes everywhere. Chocolate-filled Valentine hearts appear as soon as Santa Claus disappears. Tiny red hearts on restaurant menus sometimes serve to warn kids away from the foods their health-conscious parents prefer. For many of us, hearts also represent the love of God for his people. Every human heart is important to God. He cares about our sweethearts and our heart rates. But most of all God cares about our heart's relationship with him.

In this lesson you will see God's power working in Nehemiah's heart and life. Nehemiah's close relationship with God gave him wisdom and courage in the face of great hostility.

In 445 B.C. God sent Nehemiah to Jerusalem to confront Sanballat, Tobiah, and Geshem—Judah's enemies. Sanballat was the governor of Samaria, and Tobiah was also a Persian official. By halting the rebuilding of Jerusalem's walls, they hoped to keep Jewish political influence from developing. Geshem, a Bedouin chieftain, didn't want to share the profits of the spice trade with the Jews.

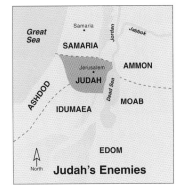

Judah's Enemies

These powerful men had successfully intimidated the people of Jerusalem. They had also kept Jerusalem's walls in ruins. Together they represent the power of evil that hates the good and opposes God's plan for his people on earth.

And then Nehemiah blew into town. He came with the authority of the king and in the power of God. With the energy and focus of a whirlwind, Nehemiah swept the people up in his enthusiasm for rebuilding the city walls. After years of delay, the people rebuilt the walls in 52 days.

Nehemiah brought hope and new life to his people. His life and work was a sign of the perfect hope that Jesus would bring many years later. Good things happened because Nehemiah's heart was in the right place.

This wall in Jerusalem follows the same line as Nehemiah's wall.

8 ▬ ▬ ▬ ➤ Celebrating God's Law

Bible Reference: Nehemiah 8–10

Way back in Old Testament times God taught the people how to celebrate holidays. He knew that to have strong human connections, we need to acknowledge our common connection to him. So the early feasts and festive days included some serious remembering of God's requirements and promises.

When Nehemiah's crew finished rebuilding Jerusalem's wall, they had a celebration. This festival included heavy-duty remembering. Ezra stood on a high wooden platform in the town square and began to read the law of

Sukkot

The Feast of Booths, sometimes called Sukkot, began in the time of Moses. During this feast the Jewish people celebrated their escape from slavery in Egypt. They also remembered God's care during their long desert journey when the tired, dusty travelers had built simple huts to shelter themselves from the scorching sun.

Many Jews still hold a week-long celebration of the Feast of Booths. In September or October they build a little booth (a *sukkah*) that they cover loosely with branches. They leave enough space to let in the light. Sometimes families even sleep in their sukkah.

They might decorate their booth with wreaths, paper chains, berries, vines, and gourds. To make it a beautiful place, they also put lovely carpets on the floor. Some Jewish people also make *lulovs* by bunching together sweet-smelling willow, myrtle, and palm branches. They also carry a lemon-like fruit called an *etrog* to symbolize God's goodness.

Another tradition is to invite family and friends to join the celebration. They also invite special biblical guests called *usppizin*. Honorary guests like Moses, David, and Sarah help them remember the story of God's goodness and faithfulness.

God. Men, women, and children stood and listened from daybreak until noon. The reading of the law continued for eight days.

During the reading of the law the people discovered a long forgotten festival called the Feast of Booths. At Mount Sinai Moses had given instructions for celebrating it. This festival's purpose was to remind the people of God's saving acts and to thank God for the harvest.

Does that sound familiar? We could say that Moses was the father of the first Thanksgiving.

9 — — — — ➤ Malachi: The End of the Beginning

Bible Reference: The Book of Malachi

Imagine that a friend talks you into going to an R-rated movie. It makes you feel extremely uncomfortable, and you hope that your parents never find out. But the next morning your mom seems upset, and you know that you're in trouble. You swallow nervously and wonder how she found out.

You can feel her eyes on you, but you look down. "You know that we have always trusted you," she begins. You stare at your cereal bowl. "Did you find a good bargain at the mall yesterday?" Your guilty face answers, and she continues. "I'm really disappointed. We didn't raise you to be a sneak." Before you have a chance to say a word, and with just a hint of sarcasm, she says, "I know what you're going to say. 'Why do you always expect the worst from me?'"

You refuse to look at her as she lists some pretty good reasons for limiting your movie attendance. You feel defensive and angry, but in your heart you know she's right.

Can you imagine trying to win an argument with God? In this lesson, there are seven arguments between God and his people. They have a statement–question–explanation pattern. First Malachi stated God's position, then he repeated the people's questions, and then he gave God's explanation. In the Bible this argumentative teaching style is called disputation. When they heard these disputation type sermons, the people knew what God wanted from them.

The first disputation reminded the people of God's love for his faithful people and his record of crushing evil. In the second and third Malachi thundered against the priests' careless, spiritless leadership. In the next three Malachi detailed the sins of all of the people. The last disputation again reminded the people of God's mercy and compassion for those who trust in his unfailing love. It also reminded them that the wicked would be judged.

Like all of the other prophets, Malachi wanted the people to let God control their hearts and lives. He wanted them to see the connection between saying that they loved God and living ethical and moral lives. He wanted them to know the depth of God's opposition to evil. And he wanted them to understand that God would go to great lengths to win control of their lives.

Malachi ends the Old Testament with a note of longing—a deep desire for the messiah to come and put things right. Although many of the Jews did not understand the nature of the coming kingdom, some turned their faces toward the sun of righteousness. From this light-filled remnant would come the light of the whole world.

Sunrise on Mount Sinai.

Unit 9
Between the Testaments

1 ━ ━ ━ ━ ━ ━ ━ ➤ Unit Overview

The Silent Years

Have you ever wondered why the Greeks were so important or where the Pharisees and Sadducees came from? Learning about what went on between the testaments helps us understand the New Testament.

The last book of the Old Testament was probably written around 400 B.C., and the first New Testament book was written around A.D. 50, leaving a span of more than 400 years between the two testaments. Although the Bible is silent about this period, God's people were still called to follow him, and God's promises were still in effect.

Sources of Information

To find out what happened to God's people during the period between the testaments, we will have to turn to other sources. We don't consider these sources to be inspired by God, but they do help us understand the history of the Jewish people.

One source is a collection of writings called the Apocrypha. These books are not part of Protestant Bibles, but they have been included in Roman Catholic Bibles ever since the 16th century. There are 12 books in the Apocrypha, almost all of them written between about 200 B.C. and the time of Christ's birth.

Another valuable source is the writings of the Jewish historian Josephus. He was born in Jerusalem in A.D. 37 and died in the early second century.

Flavius Josephus.

Among his writings are *The Jewish Wars* and *Antiquities of the Jews*, a complete history of the Jews from the time of Moses through his own lifetime that is 20 volumes long.

The Persian Period (539–330 B.C.)

At the beginning of the period between the testaments, Persia was the world power. As we have seen, the rulers of the Persian Empire were very tolerant of varying beliefs. The Jews were allowed to control themselves without interference. Their high priests were in charge of religious and civil affairs. Cyrus, Darius, and Artaxerxes even helped the Jews in their efforts to rebuild. As long as Judah paid its taxes and didn't rebel, the Persian rulers were content.

Greek (Hellenistic) Period (330–166 B.C.)

Alexander the Great

The great Persian empire fell to Alexander the Great. His well-trained army flattened the Persian forces, and he seized control of Palestine in 332 B.C. During a period of seven years Alexander conquered almost the whole known world. According to a legend, he wept because there were no more worlds to conquer.

One of Alexander's goals was to spread Greek culture and language to his whole empire. Actually, he was a Macedonian, not a Greek. But he believed in the Greek way of life called Hellenism.

The Empire Splits

In 323 B.C. when Alexander was only 33 years old, he became ill and died. Alexander's generals took control. They began struggling for power, and soon the empire was split. The two most powerful generals were Ptolemy and Seleucus. Ptolemy controlled Egypt; Seleucus controlled the eastern part of the empire. Both wanted to control the important trade routes that crossed Palestine, so the Jews were caught in the middle. Sometimes they were ruled by the Ptolemies and sometimes by the Seleucids.

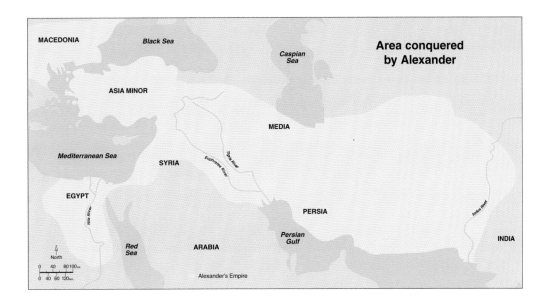

The Ptolemies were in control of Palestine from around 300 to 200 B.C., and the Jews lived in peace. But in 198 B.C. the Seleucids defeated the army of the Ptolemies and took control of Palestine. This turned out to be bad news for the Jews. At first things were fine, but when Antiochus Epiphanes took the throne, trouble began. His policies were so oppressive that the Jews finally rebelled.

Hasmonean Period (166–63 B.C.)

The oppression by the Seleucids led to an open revolt led by Judas Maccabeus. After years of struggle, the Jews became independent in 142 B.C. During the next ten years their nation grew in size until it equalled the size of Solomon's kingdom. The Maccabees set up a dynasty called the Hasmonean dynasty (they were descendants of Asamoneus or Hasmon).

The Roman Period (63 B.C.–A.D. 37)

The next empire to dominate the world scene was the Roman Empire. The Romans had been flexing their muscles for some time. They had pushed Antiochus Epiphanes, the Seleucid, out of Egypt in 168 B.C. The Romans continued to expand their empire and, in 63 B.C., under the leadership of Pompey, they conquered Judah and Jerusalem.

These are the books most commonly called the Apocrypha. Written between about 300 B.C. and A.D. 100, they span the gap between the Old and New Testaments. Christians disagree over the exact status of these books. Are they part of inspired Scripture or not?

Roman Catholics say yes to this, although they call the books 'deuterocanonical,' which means that they are drawn from a second list of 'canonical' (authoritative) books. In Catholic Bibles these books are scattered in appropriate places throughout the Old Testament.

Protestants say no. They believe that the books are not part of Scripture, but that they are useful for reading by Christians. In Protestant Bibles, the Apocrypha is either left out completely or appears in a block between the Old and New Testaments.

Christians are agreed that the books of the Apocrypha, carefully read, are valuable in linking the history of the Old and New Testaments and also for their wisdom and spiritual insight.

In 37 B.C. the Romans put Herod in power in Jerusalem. Herod's ancestors were Edomites (descendants of Esau and ancient enemies of the Jews), so the Jews disliked him from the start. This is the King Herod who ordered the murder of the baby boys in Bethlehem in an attempt to kill the Christ child. The Jews of Christ's day hated Roman rule, and they hated Herod.

2 ▬ ▬ ▬ ▬ ➤ Time to Learn Greek

When Alexander marched out of Greece and successfully conquered Persia, he brought more than his army with him. He brought along a whole way of life. Alexander had a dream. His dream was to unite the world's people by spreading Greek culture (Hellenism).

Alexander set about making his dream come true by establishing Greek colonies throughout the world. Each of these colonies became a center from which Greek culture gradually spread out. Alexander established more than 60 cities for this purpose. The most famous city he founded was Alexandria, Egypt. It became a great center of the Greek culture.

What was happening to the Jews during this time? Did they stay away from these Greek cities and Greek influence?

The Dispersion

God's people, the Jews, were no longer a tight little group living in Palestine. In fact, by this time most of them were no longer living in Palestine. They were scattered all over the Greek empire. Many had not returned from exile but had settled in cities in the Persian empire. From there they had moved to other places.

During the time between the testaments, still more Jews moved to cities throughout the Greek empire. Alexandria, Egypt, for example, became a world center for Jews. These Jews who lived outside of Palestine and yet maintained

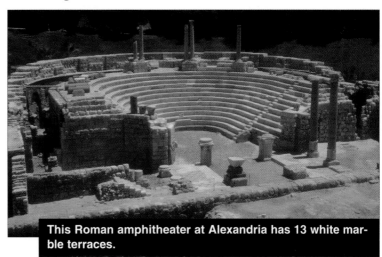

This Roman amphitheater at Alexandria has 13 white marble terraces.

their religion are called the Diaspora or Jews of the dispersion. (The word *disperse* means "to scatter on all sides"; the Greek word *diaspora* means "that which is sown, like seed.")

The Influence of Hellenism

This worldwide scattering of Jews was a very important development in the story of God's people. The faithful Jews were waiting for the messiah. So when Paul and other Christians came to them with news of Jesus, many were open to the gospel. Naturally, these Jews of the dispersion were greatly influenced by Greek ways. Many of them were traders and merchants, so they had to learn the Greek language in order to keep their businesses running. But merchants weren't the only Jews learning Greek. Any Jew who wanted to be successful had to learn Greek. It was the language of the empire.

Jews of the dispersion adopted more than the Greek language. Jewish youths raced in the popular Greek games. Jews enjoyed Greek plays; some even wrote plays for the Greek stage. Jews studied Greek philosophy; some Jewish philosophers even tried to show how Greek thinking matched the thoughts of Moses. Jews also copied Greek architecture; many Jewish buildings copied Greek designs and forms.

What about Religion?

You can probably see where all of this is leading. The Greeks believed in more than a dozen gods: Zeus (the father of the Greek gods), Hera, Athena,

Apollo by Girardon, 1666.

Apollo, Venus, Mars, and more. They built temples to their gods and brought them offerings. Their religion was far different from that of the Jews, who were supposed to worship the one, true God and keep his law. Yet some Jews tried to fit Greek beliefs into their religion. And not just the Jews of the dispersion; even in Jerusalem many Jews became like the Greeks in their thinking, lifestyle, and religion.

A Soft, Subtle Pressure

The Greeks didn't order others to accept their ways and beliefs. But the pressure was there. It came from within. We all know how important it is to fit in. The Jews, too, wanted to be liked and accepted by their friends—even if they had to change some of their customs or beliefs.

This subtle pressure was more dangerous than direct pressure. If the Jews had been persecuted, they might have resisted. They might have seen the danger and held onto their religion and way of life even tighter. But many Jews in Palestine and throughout the Greek empire were influenced by Hellenism. Only the most faithful held on to the religion of their parents.

Alexandria and the Septuagint

The language of the Jews in Egypt was Greek. And as time went on, few Jews could understand Hebrew. That meant that most of the Jews could no longer understand the Scriptures. So Jewish scholars started translating the Scriptures into Greek. Around 250 B.C. only the Pentateuch was translated into Greek. But by 120 B.C. the other Old Testament books had also been translated.

This Greek translation came to be called the Septuagint. The Septuagint was the greatest contribution of the Alexandrian Jews. Now not only Greek-speaking Jews but also Gentiles could read the Scriptures. So, as it turned out, the Greek language—part of the influence of Hellenism—helped spread the influence of Judaism.

The Septuagint

The word *Septuagint* comes from the Latin word for 70. Often the Roman numeral LXX is used to refer to the Septuagint. According to legend, 72 Jewish scholars working in 72 separate cells worked on this translation. At the end of 72 days they compared their translations and found that all versions were exactly alike. Some legends even claim that these translators completed the entire Old Testament in these 72 days!

Ruins of a medieval fort on Pharos Island, Alexandria, where the Septuagint was most likely written.

3 ━ ➤ In the Middle of a Tug-of-War

The Land Between

Following the death of Alexander the Great, Palestine again became a battleground. Remember that Palestine is only about 150 miles long and 50–60 miles wide. Why do you think nations would fight over this little strip of land?

The answer lies in the location of Palestine and the land features of the area. On the west side is the Mediterranean Sea; on the south lies a nearly impassible desert. Much of the center of Palestine is mountainous. All of this means that there were only a couple of routes through the heart of Palestine. These routes connected competing empires. The Egyptians in north Africa were ancient rivals of the Asian empires to the north and east of Palestine. Powerful Persian and Babylonian armies battered Palestine as they fought with Egypt for control of trade and territory.

The Ptolemies and the Seleucids

Alexander's dream of a peaceful, united world turned into a nightmare for the people of Palestine after his death. The Greek empire was divided between two ruling families: the Ptolemies and the Seleucids. The Ptolemies controlled the southern part; their capital was in Egypt. The Seleucids controlled the northern and eastern parts; their capital was in Syria. In between them was Palestine, which both the Ptolemies and Seleucids wanted to control.

From 323–198 B.C. the Ptolemies controlled Palestine. They were tolerant, allowing the Jews to live and worship as they pleased. The pressure of Hellenism was there, but it was soft and subtle.

But the situation changed when Antiochus the Great became the Seleucid ruler. He tried to take Palestine away from the Ptolemies in a series of battles. The Jews were caught in the middle of this tug-of-war and suf-

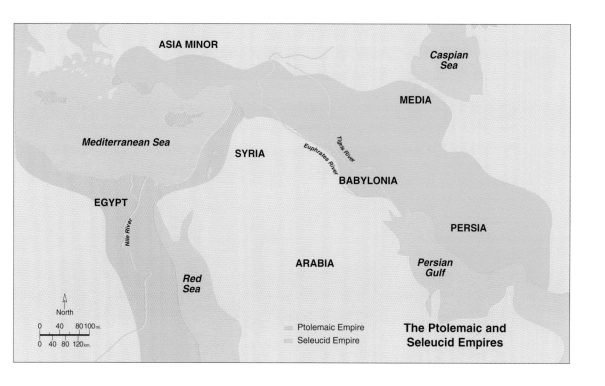

The Ptolemaic and
Seleucid Empires

fered greatly. Finally, in 198 B.C. in a battle in northern Palestine, the Seleucids smashed the Ptolemy army and pushed it out of Palestine.

Even though the Ptolemies had been tolerant, the Jews welcomed Antiochus the Great into Jerusalem. They were happy to see the war between the Ptolemies and Seleucids ended. And they hoped the Seleucids would be even more gracious then the Ptolemies. And they were—for a while. Antiochus released some Jewish captives. He delayed the payment of taxes in Jerusalem for three years to give the people opportunity to recover from the war. In fact, Antiochus the Great decreed that the Jews could live according to their old laws.

Growing Roman Power

But the good times didn't last, because the Roman Empire was beginning to muscle its way to power. When Antiochus tried to conquer Greece in 190 B.C., a powerful Roman army smashed the Seleucid forces. To further humiliate Antiochus, the Romans held his son hostage in Rome for 12 years. They demanded such heavy taxes from the Seleucids that one day

Some scholars say that Antiochus tangled with the Romans because he sheltered Hannibal, a North African general from the city of Carthage. Hannibal had escaped to the protection of Antiochus after the Romans had routed his army. Hannibal then persuaded the Seleucids to invade Greece. Like Hannibal, the Seleucids used elephants for combat. And like Hannibal, the Seleucids were defeated by the Romans. They lost the war and they lost their elephant "tanks."

The Battle, unknown Italian artist, 15th century.

Antiochus tried to rob a temple to pay his Roman tax bill. That desperate act led to his death.

After this, the Seleucid empire gradually declined. Its rulers, always short of money, began to make heavier demands on the people. Antiochus Epiphanes—the son who had been held hostage by the Romans—took the throne. Under him the tolerant attitude toward the Jews disappeared. His goal was to force the Jews to drop their religion and customs and to accept Hellenism completely. And he was determined to do whatever it took to accomplish his goal.

4 ━ ━ ━ ━ ━ ➤ Antiochus IV, Epiphanes or Epimanes?

How the Crisis Developed

When Antiochus Epiphanes came to the Seleucid throne in 175 B.C., he had high hopes of Hellenizing his kingdom. His hostility to orthodox Judaism created an enormous crisis for the Jews. Although this crisis had been brewing for more than 100 years, Antiochus brought it to a head. His last name—Epiphanes—tells us something about him; it means "the god manifest." In other words, he claimed to be a god. Actually, he claimed to be the visible presence of the god Zeus. The Jews came to hate him and gave him the nickname Epimanes, meaning "madman." Let's see how the crisis developed and how the Jews came to despise Antiochus.

Many Jews throughout the empire had enthusiastically accepted Greek culture. They were called Hellenists. But a group of faithful and devout Jews had always resisted Hellenism. They were passionately committed to God's law, and they stubbornly resisted any attempts to change traditional patterns of life and worship. Eventually this deeply religious group was called the Hasidim, meaning "faithful ones."

The seething bitterness between Hellenistic Jews and the Hasidim erupted into a full-fledged brawl over one key issue, the office of high priest. During the golden days of Israel's kings, the role of high priest was strictly religious. The high priest's most important function was to offer sacrifices on behalf of the people. Each year on the Day of Atonement he sacrificed flawless animals to win forgiveness for the sins of the people. This also reminded the people of God's gracious forgiveness for those who repented and turned their hearts to him.

The role of the high priest changed following the exile. Persian and Seleucid rulers did not allow the Jews to have a king. So the high priest took on political responsibilities along with his obligations of religious leadership. Whoever filled the position of high priest had great power.

When Antiochus began to control Palestine, a devoutly religious Levite,

Hannah and Her Sons: A Jewish Story

Long ago, during the days of the Maccabean revolt against the cruel Seleucids, there lived a deeply religious woman named Hannah. She raised her seven sons to love and honor God. Antiochus ordered her sons executed for worshiping God and refusing to bow to the Greek gods. Before each son was executed, Hannah comforted them with these words: "As God blessed you with life in this world, so he will bless you with eternal life." Antiochus tried to persuade her youngest son to deny his allegiance to God, but the youngest son refused. Hannah comforted him with these words: "My son, go to your death with honor, trusting in God as your brothers did, so that we may all be reunited when the time of redemption comes." Before he was tortured and executed, the boy addressed Antiochus, "We know that though we suffer now, God will yet be merciful with us and has granted us eternal life. But you will suffer greatly for your tyranny, and will never escape divine punishment."

Onias III, was high priest. Antiochus correctly identified Onias as his most powerful opponent and decided to remove him from power. Antiochus hoped to achieve this by putting the office of high priest up for sale. If he could sell the office of high priest to the highest bidder, he would gain two things. Antiochus would probably raise a heap of money for his starving treasury and would also get rid of Onias so that he could install a Hellenistic high priest. To religious Jews selling the office of high priest was an outrageous sin against God. The Hellenistic Jews saw it as a great opportunity to secure favor with the Seleucid king.

What Happened Next?

Onias had a brother named Jason. Jason's enthusiasm for Greek culture was as fervent as Onias's devotion to Judaism. Jason's generous bribe to Antiochus gave him the high priestly office and a great opportunity to Hellenize his fellow Jews. Jason showed contempt for God and for the religious aspect of his office when he allowed a gymnasium to be built near the temple in Jerusalem. A sports center might seem innocent to us, but Greek sports were closely connected to various Greek gods. By participating in these activities, an athlete acknowledged the authority and protection of the Greek gods. He also rejected God's laws and moral requirements.

Jason managed to keep his job as high priest until one of his associates, Menelaus, outbid him. To the Hasidim, Menelaus was worse than Jason. For one thing he was not a Levite; he was from the tribe of Benjamin. He also sold some of the golden temple vessels. When Onias objected, Menelaus had him killed. Then Jason jumped back into the competition. He fought Menelaus with 1,000 soldiers but couldn't unseat him. The chaos in Jerusalem attracted Antiochus's attention.

Antiochus Joins the Fracas

On his way back from Egypt, Antiochus stopped off in Jerusalem to straighten out the Jews. He did it with a vengeance. According to Josephus, Antiochus "personally led a great army and captured the city. . . . He himself despoiled the temple treasury and forbade the practice of daily sacrifice for three years and six months."

In 168 B.C. the Romans humiliated Antiochus and drove his army out of Egypt. He was still smarting from this defeat when he heard that some Jews were still ignoring his command to "turn Greek." In response he sent an army into Judea to teach them a lesson. Appolonius, the general in charge, knew that the Jews wouldn't fight on the Sabbath. So he attacked on the Sabbath without

This is where the Jewish revolt against Antiochus Epiphanes began. The burial chambers here at Modiin are topped with heavy blocks.

warning. His soldiers killed many people, looted Jerusalem, and tore down the walls. Then they built a new fortress for the Seleucid soldiers.

To make matters worse, Antiochus issued a new set of orders making the Jewish religion illegal. There could be no sacrifices, no circumcision, and no Sabbath worship. Copies of the law were burned. Jews were ordered to worship Greek gods and were forced to eat pig meat, which they considered unclean. And worst of all, the Lord God of Israel was identified with the Greek god Zeus. As a final abomination, pigs were sacrificed on the altar in the temple.

The authorities enforced Antiochus's orders with harsh cruelty. When an old scribe named Eleazar refused to eat pig meat, he was flogged to death. The only Jews to be spared were the ones who were willing to renounce their faith in God. The situation couldn't have been worse.

5 ▬ ▬ ▬ ➤ The Feast of Dedication

Hasidim Resistance

Antiochus Epiphanes did not let up on his persecution of Jews who insisted on obeying God's law. But the harder he tried to stamp out their religion, the more the Jewish people resisted. Leading the resistance was a group called the Hasidim—the pious or loyal ones. The Hasidim were mostly common country people. But a few rich and upper-class people also joined. The Hasidim hated and resisted Hellenism and other foreign influences. That's what they were against.

Centering on the Torah

Here's what the Hasidim were for. They were for the law of God found in the first five books of the Bible, which they called the Torah. The Torah became the center and the symbol of their religion. This devotion to the Torah may have started during the time of the exile when there was no temple. For the exiles and for the Jews of the dispersion the only symbol of their religion was the sacred Scriptures. The Jewish love for the Torah grew even more in this time of persecution. To defend the Torah was to defend their faith.

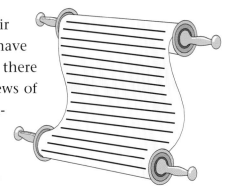

A Priest Revolts

Antiochus must have been aware of the Jews' devotion to the Torah. He and the Hasidim were on a collision course. Then something with far-reaching results happened in an out-of-the-way place in Judah. Here's what might have happened, based on 1 Maccabees 2:17–22.

Narrator: The king's officers came to Modiin, a town not far from Jerusalem. Their mission was to get the Jews to cooperate with the king's order to worship Greek gods. They decided to try to win over a key leader, the priest Mattathias.

King's officer 1: Greetings, Mattathias. I'm glad we found you here. Isn't it a beautiful day? It's good to see so many of your people gathered here.

Mattathias (*briskly*): Good morning. What can I do for you?

King's officer 2: Well, you surely don't waste any words!

Mattathias: You're right. I think I know what you're here for, so you can forget the small talk.

King's officer 2: All right then; I won't beat around the bush. We've come because we know that people around here respect you and will do whatever you tell them to do.

King's officer 1: And your sons are so capable—and loved by the people.

Mattathias: You can cut the flattery too!

King's officer 1: Don't be so touchy. Antiochus thinks you can persuade the people to be a little more cooperative. All you have to do is . . . uh . . . offer a little sacrifice to Zeus.

Mattathias: To Zeus? You must be crazy!

King's officer 1: Now take it easy, Mattathias. It doesn't matter what name you give to God. All you have to do is tell the people that Zeus is another name for Yahweh. They won't care.

King's officer 2: Besides, there's a little something special in this for you. Antiochus authorized me to offer you a nice gift in exchange for your cooperation. You and your sons will be enrolled in the elite club called "The Friends of the King."

King's officer 1: We'll make it worth your while. What do you say, Mattathias?

Mattathias (*loudly and forcefully*): I don't care what anyone else is doing. If they abandon their gods and their religion, that's their business. My sons and I will never play your little game.

Judas: Don't even think of mentioning Zeus in this place again. We will never abandon the covenant or God's laws.

Jonathan: We'll never obey the king's command to sacrifice to Zeus or any other Greek god.

King's officer 2: You don't know what you're refusing: a grand house, travel, a nice fat bank account.

Judas: You just don't understand. Without our religion, our lives have no real meaning.

King's officer 1: Is that your last word? Is that what you want us to . . .

Hellenistic Jew (*interrupting*): Wait a minute. Don't go. Mattathias doesn't speak for all of us. Is that gift package you offered transferrable to me and my boys? Bring that squealing little pig to me. I'll sacrifice him for you. No problem.

Mattathias: Don't even think of it, traitor! There is a problem. If you even try to sacrifice to that heathen god, you will die.

Narrator: Before the traitor could begin the sacrifice, Mattathias slaughtered him and then killed one of the king's officers. Mattathias recruited others to join him and, fearing the anger of Antiochus, they fled to the hills.

The Growing Rebellion

Many people did follow Mattathias—especially the Hasidim. From then on, the rebellion grew. Mattathias and his rebels raided towns and villages—destroying pagan altars and killing the king's soldiers and the Jews who supported the king. Mattathias soon died, but his third son, Judas Maccabeus (meaning "the hammer") followed him as the rebels' leader (166 B.C.). More Jews rallied to the cause.

Since Antiochus had other revolts to put down at the same time, he couldn't send a large army to deal with the problem in Judea. The forces he did send were met and defeated by Judas Maccabeus and his followers. Then in 164 B.C., after they won a battle against the Seleucids in Judah, the rebels marched to Jerusalem.

What did they find? The temple was in a terrible state: the altar had been desecrated, the gates were burned down, the courts were overgrown "like a thicket," and the priests' rooms were ruined. "They tore their garments, wailed loudly, put ashes on their heads and fell on their faces to the ground" (1 Maccabees 4:39).

Then the Maccabees set about cleansing the temple. First they destroyed the pagan altar. Then they rebuilt and restored the temple. A sweet fragrance filled the temple when they burned incense on the new altar. They relit the lamps, and once again light from the sacred lamps burned brightly in the temple.

Celebrating Hanukkah—the Feast of Dedication

On the 25th day of the Jewish month of Kislev (November-December) the Jews rededicated the temple altar and held a joyful eight-day celebration. They brought burnt offerings, peace offerings, and thank offerings. They even decorated the front of the temple with golden wreaths.

Then "Judas, his brothers, and the whole congregation of Israel decreed that the rededication of the altar should be observed with joy and gladness at the same season each year, for eight days, beginning on the twenty-fifth of Kislev" (1 Maccabees 4:59). And that's how the Jewish holiday of Hanukkah—meaning "dedication"—began.

Today one of the special symbols of Hanukkah is the menorah, a candlestick that holds nine candles, one for each day of the celebration and a center one that is used to light the others. The first candle is lit on the first

The Feast of Dedication is also called the Feast of Lights. This name recalls the relighting of the temple lamp. According to legend, the Jews could find only enough consecrated oil to keep the lamp burning for one day. But they lit the lamp anyway, and—by a miracle—the lamp continued to burn for eight days. Then more oil was available.

night of Hanukkah. On the next night, two candles are lit. On the third night, three candles, and so on, until all eight are lit on the last night.

The Feast of Dedication is, of course, a Jewish celebration, but the event it celebrates is also important for Christians. It helped prepare the way for Jesus to be born. So, let's be thankful for the success of the Jewish rebellion and the cleansing of the temple in 164 B.C.

6 — — ➤ The Rise of Roman Power

Have you ever been surprised when playing a game that requires strategy? You were so busy trying to keep ahead of your opponent that you didn't notice another danger growing somewhere else. That's what happened to the Hasmonean (descendants of the Maccabees) rulers of Judea. They were so busy fighting each other and trying to escape the clutches of the cruel Seleucids that they didn't recognize the growing menace of the Roman war machine.

While the Hasmoneans were struggling to control Palestine, the Roman Empire was expanding and spreading toward them. In 146 B.C., sometime after Judas Maccabeus died, the Romans completely destroyed Carthage,

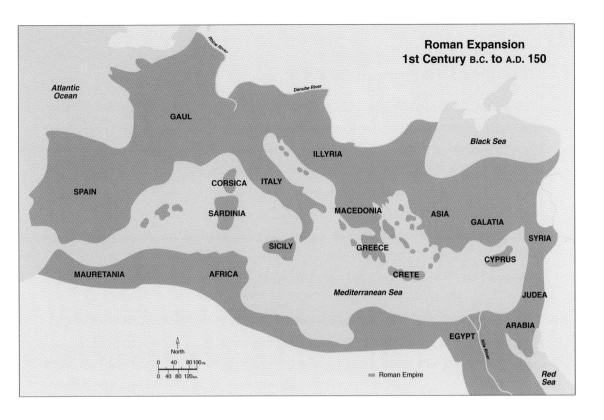

Atlantic Ocean

Rhine River

GAUL

Danube River

ILLYRIA

Black Sea

SPAIN

CORSICA ITALY

MACEDONIA

ASIA

GALATIA

SARDINIA

SYRIA

SICILY

GREECE

CYPRUS

MAURETANIA

AFRICA

CRETE

Mediterranean Sea

JUDEA

ARABIA

EGYPT

Nile River

North

0   40   80 100 m.
0 40 80 120 km.

Roman Empire

Red Sea

which they had been fighting against for over 100 years. With Carthage out of the picture, the Romans were free to move into the eastern Mediterranean region. While this Roman expansion was going on, the Jews in Judea had a period of relative peace under the high priests Simon and John Hyrcanus. After the death of Hyrcanus, there was a long period of civil unrest that lasted until the Roman invasion.

Sibling Rivalry

Toward the end of this period two brothers, Aristobulus II and Hyrcanus II, who were descendants of Simon Maccabeus, were fighting for the right to rule the country. A Roman general, Pompey, saw this as an opportunity for Rome to step into Jewish affairs. He offered to get to the bottom of the conflict and turned his army toward Jerusalem. The brothers continued to fight each other even as the Roman army approached. Both groups eventually retreated to Jerusalem. Hyrcanus's followers, however, opened the gates for Pompey, while the followers of Aristobulus held out in the temple area.

Pompey Conquers Jerusalem

Pompey laid siege to the temple area. He had to fill the valley below the wall of the temple with dirt in order to bring his battering rams up against the walls. Hyrcanus's people gave Pompey advice and help. Pompey also cleverly used the Jewish Sabbath to his advantage. Because the Jews only fought in self-defense on the Sabbath, Pompey had his men work on filling in the valley on the Sabbath. In this way Pompey finally positioned his battering rams and broke down the wall. Josephus tells us that the towers were massive and resisted the battering for a long time. When the Romans finally broke into the temple area, a terrible fight followed. Twelve thousand Jews died in the battle.

According to the account of Josephus in *The Jewish Wars*, "Pompey was amazed at the unshakable endurance of the Jews, and more particularly at their uninterrupted maintenance of religious practices in the midst of a hail of missiles. . . . On the very day the Temple was captured, when they were being slain around the sacrificial altar, they never abandoned the rites ordained for the day."

Pompey may have been impressed by the Jews' actions, but the Jews were horrified by his. Pompey entered the Most Holy Place of the temple. He saw the costly furnishings as well as a treasury of 2,000 talents. But Pompey didn't plunder the temple treasures. He even ordered the temple sacrifices to be resumed.

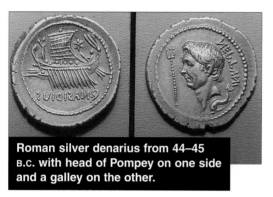

Roman silver denarius from 44–45 B.C. with head of Pompey on one side and a galley on the other.

Judea was now part of the Roman Empire. The year was 63 B.C. Pompey repaid Hyrancus II for his cooperation by making him governor and also allowing him to be the high priest.

Antipater's Plan

During the Judean power struggle, Hyrcanus got help not only from the

Romans but also from the Idumeans, who lived below the Dead Sea. The Idumeans were Edomites, descendants of Esau. The Idumean king who helped Hyrcanus was Antipater. In fact, Antipater became the real power behind Hyrcanus. Because of the long history of hatred and rivalry between Jews and Edomites, the Jews bitterly resented both the Idumeans and Antipater. Antipater wasn't concerned about their history of bad blood. He wanted to increase his area of influence. Besides, he was looking for powerful positions for his sons. One of his sons was Herod.

The Reign of Herod

Herod tried to win the confidence and goodwill of the Jewish people, but he was more eager for the confidence and goodwill of the Roman rulers. Herod switched loyalties to whichever party he thought would win in Rome. In 37 B.C. the Romans gave him the title "King of the Jews" and helped him win the throne. Herod reigned there until 4 B.C. He was the ruler who tried to kill the child Jesus in Bethlehem. Only after his death did Joseph and Mary dare to return to Palestine.

7 ------➤ The Pharisees: Lovers of the Law

It wasn't long ago that many Christians had strict rules banning "worldly amusements." Card-playing, dancing, and drinking alcohol were forbidden. So was movie attendance and playing sports on Sunday. Devout Christians wanted to preserve their strong, healthy identity as God's children. For some Christians the rules that were intended to strengthen their Christian identity became the focus of their Christianity. They spent more energy judging others' actions than praising God. For them, the rules became the heart of their religion.

The Pharisees Conspire Together by James J. Tissot, 1836–1902.

Something similar happened to the Jews facing the pressure to adopt Hellenism. They saw their fellow Jews ignoring God's law, and they experienced enormous pressure to abandon their religious traditions. In response they fervently defended and promoted God's law. Their devotion to the law had an unforeseen effect on Jewish religious life. The Jewish leaders called Pharisees began to lose sight of the other requirements of the covenant. The rituals surrounding worship faded as the law became the center of religion for the Jews.

The Hasidim Split from the Maccabees

The Pharisees originated from the Hasidim, the group of Jews that opposed Hellenism. Toward the end of the Maccabean revolt and during the years of independence, the Hasidim withdrew their support from the Maccabees. One objection of the Hasidim was that the Maccabees seemed more interested in gaining political power than in upholding their religion. The Hasidim also objected when the later Maccabeans became high priests. Although the Maccabeans came from Aaron's line, they were not descendants of Zadok. David had specifically said that only men from the family of Zadok could hold the office of high priest. When the Maccabeans began to distort the law for their own purposes, the Hasidim split off.

The Hasidim Split

Within the Hasidim there were differences of opinion as well. So during the Hasmonean period, the Hasidim split into two groups. One group—the Essenes—wanted to completely separate themselves from any Hellenistic influence by physically separating themselves from Jerusalem. Many of the members of this group moved into the wilderness to protest what was going on in Judah and Jerusalem.

The second group—the Pharisees—stayed in Jerusalem and other Judean cities. The first mention of the Pharisees occurs during the reign of the Hasmonean John Hyrcanus (134–104 B.C.). The word *Pharisee* means "separated ones." The name probably referred to the group's desire to separate from Hellenism or from anything foreign. The Pharisees built up a wall of traditions to keep out Hellenistic influences.

The Importance of God's Law

The Essenes and the Pharisees both believed that the fall of Jerusalem in 586 B.C. and the Babylonian exile took place because the Jews failed to follow God's law. Because the Pharisees didn't want to fall into the sins of their ancestors by adopting pagan Hellenistic ways, they tried to strictly follow all the laws of Moses. Observing all these laws was difficult because it wasn't always easy for people to interpret each law in different situations.

Understanding the Law

The Pharisees thought they knew how to interpret the Ten Commandments and every other law of the Pentateuch. The Pharisees continued through the years to apply the hundreds of laws to new situations. The right behavior in each new situation was decided by studying and quoting what well-known rabbis had said about the issue in the past. For example:

"Rabbi Hillel says that we are commanded by God to care for the fatherless, the widows and orphans."

"Rabbi Shammai says that if there are two men and only one gives to the poor, there is really only one man—the other is a dog."

What the rabbis said was passed from one generation to another by word of mouth. These teachings, passed on orally, are called the oral tradition. When Jesus as a young boy was in the temple talking with the rabbis, he was probably discussing these teachings with them.

Legalism Long Ago

The oral tradition eventually became more than just traditions or comments on the law. The Pharisees taught people to obey these oral laws even more strictly than the law of Moses. They believed that their oral interpretations applied more directly to the lives of the people. The Pharisees argued that if the people kept the oral laws strictly, they wouldn't even come close to breaking the written law of Moses. They saw the oral interpretations as a kind of fence that protected the law and protected the people from the bad influences of their culture. Many years after Jesus' life on earth, the Pharisees began to collect these oral interpretations. They wrote them in a book called the MISHNA.

The Pharisees were dedicated leaders, urging the people to be faithful to the covenant. Their desire to resist Hellenism was good, but they began to worship their interpretation of the law instead of using God's law to worship God. When rules start to take the place of God in our lives, it is called *legalism*.

Legalism Today

Do you think that legalism is a serious problem today? Do people spend a great deal of time trying to figure out whether they are keeping God's rules correctly? Some Christian communities still resist the influence of modern culture by cutting themselves off from worldly amusements and entertainment. They don't watch television, and they don't attend major league sports events. They live by a fairly rigid set of rules interpreting God's will for their lives. Other Christians appear to be no different from non-Christians. Their clothing, leisure activities, and favorite musicians are no different from non-Christians. Which do you think is more threatening to the Christian community today, conformity to our culture or legalism?

8 ━ ━ ━ ━ ➤ The Sadducees: The Ruling Aristocracy

Who Were They, and Where Did They Come From?

When Jesus talked about his main opponents, many times he spoke about the Pharisees and the Sadducees. He was often quite critical of both groups, and so we often think that they were alike. But almost the only thing they agreed on was their hostility to Jesus and his message. Combining Pharisees and Sadducees is something like combining liberals and conservatives. That's how different they were. You already know a little about the Pharisees, but what about the Sadducees? In the second century B.C., during the Maccabean times, the Sadducees, arose. This faction was made up of the Jewish aristocracy—the upper, ruling class—and priestly families.

What Did They Believe?

The Sadducees were sympathetic to Hellenism, and they wanted no part of the revolt led by the Maccabees. They urged cooperation with those in authority—whoever that authority was, because keeping things running smoothly and keeping foreign rulers content meant keeping their wealth and positions of power. They were not looking forward to the coming of a messiah who would set up a kingdom of peace and justice. They were satisfied with the present!

Another difference between the Pharisees and the Sadducees was in their attitude to the law. The Sadducees followed only the written Pentateuch or Torah. They rejected the oral interpretations of the Pharisees. In addition, they denied the Pharisees' belief in a future resurrection or judgment—probably because these teachings were not found in the law.

The Sadducees and Government

The Sadducees were powerful members of the Sanhedrin, the ruling council of the Jews. The exact origin of the Sanhedrin is not known, but we do know that the Greeks allowed the Jews to set up a council of elders. It was made up of aristocratic Jewish leaders; the high priest was its leader. Under the Greeks, this council had the freedom to govern Judah. This council later developed into the Sanhedrin.

Over the years the influence and makeup of the Sanhedrin changed, depending on the ruling power in the land. In the second century B.C. most of the members of the Sanhedrin were Sadducees. They could influence the civil laws of the Hasmonean rulers. But during the first century B.C., the ruling Hasmoneans allowed Pharisees to enter the Sanhedrin. The Pharisees and Sadducees continued to share the power into New Testament times. Do you think that their government meetings went smoothly?

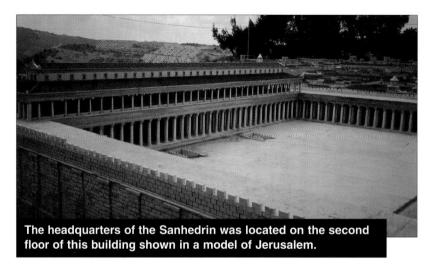

The headquarters of the Sanhedrin was located on the second floor of this building shown in a model of Jerusalem.

One way that Hellenism influenced the Pharisees was in the way that they trained teachers. In Greek cities a group of students would gather around a teacher and follow him wherever he went. As they went from place to place, they would learn by asking questions. The teacher would ask them questions in return.

The Jews adopted this format for training teachers of the law. After a student had learned enough, the teacher would lay hands on him to show that he had graduated. He could then wear a long scholarly robe and answer questions about the law. He would be a rabbi.

9 ➡ The Essenes and the Zealots: Two Extremes

The Pharisees and the Sadducees were two Jewish factions with quite different reactions to the pressure of Hellenism. But there were two other groups who didn't agree with either of them. They were the Essenes and the Zealots. They didn't agree with each other either. Most of the Essenes tried to escape Hellenism by totally separating themselves from Jewish life. They took extreme measures to stay pure and clean. If they accidentally touched someone who was not a full-fledged member, they immediately bathed to remove the pollution. The Zealots had a different response. They wanted to fight instead of escape. In this lesson you will find out more about life as an Essene and the fury of the Zealots.

The Essenes

Beginnings

The Essenes' roots were in the Hasidim of the Hasmonean period. Like the Pharisees, the Essenes wanted to resist the influence of Hellenism. But they disagreed with the Pharisees about how to resist. The Essenes thought that the best way to resist was to physically withdraw. The Pharisees also believed in separating themselves, but only by the way they lived, not by physically separating themselves.

The Essenes first lived in their own communities in Jerusalem and other cities in Palestine. Then sometime around 100 B.C. they set up settlements in the desert area near the Dead Sea. The settlement in Qumran is perhaps the most well-known, and some scholars think that it was the headquarters of the Essenes.

Finding Qumran

Qumran is right along the coast of the Dead Sea, not far from Jerusalem. Qumran is still a unique place. Imagine that you are heading east by car from Jerusalem towards the Dead Sea. The road winds downhill. In fact, you're dropping almost a mile in altitude within a half an hour. But just as the altitude drops drastically, the temperature rises drastically. From spring to fall, it is hot here already at 10 A.M. The Dead Sea is the lowest place on earth, about 1,200 feet below sea level! It's quiet and peaceful. The ground is rocky with only a little vegetation—some scrub grasses and bushes. With

Looking west at the Essene community and Qumran cliffs.

the Dead Sea at your back and looking west, you see barren limestone cliffs running north to south. In the fissures or cracks in the cliffs, you may see some discoloration—evidence that when it does rain in Jerusalem, some of the water runs in this direction. You are standing in the Rift Valley. Sometime in the past an earthquake split the earth, and the land dropped below sea level. The crack or fissure five miles south of the northern tip of the Dead Sea is Wadi Qumran. (A wadi is a dry riverbed.) If you head west towards the cliffs and walk over the scrub grass for about a mile, you see the ruins of some buildings—ancient Qumran.

Life in an Essene Community

Approximately 200 people probably lived in the Essene community at Qumran. They lived a communal life—owning the property together, worshiping together, studying together, and eating together. Their life was simple and disciplined. Josephus tells us that their day began before sunrise with morning prayers. Then each member of the community worked at an assigned task until noon. At noon they bathed and ate. Then they went back to work until evening. They studied the Scriptures every day.

Members of the community may not have been allowed to marry. Skeletons of women and children found at Qumran's cemetery show that they were also part of the community; however, we're not sure what role women and children had. Josephus wrote that the Essenes didn't like marriage, but they accepted young children into the community since they were teachable.

The Essenes linked purity of the body to purity of the soul. Archaeologists have found remains of bathing basins called mikvehs at Qumran. An Essene living at Qumran would have used a mikveh every day for personal cleansing.

Possibly a ritual bath for the Essenes at Qumran.

Initiation

Essene communities were not easy to join. There was a long and demanding initiation process. The first year would-be members had to live in very harsh conditions outside the boundaries of the community. After that they were allowed in the community on probation. After two years if they were able to keep all the rules and live up to the standards of the community, they were admitted as full members and finally allowed to join in the common meals.

The Zealots

The Zealots believed in the violent overthrow of foreign rule. Their name comes from a Hebrew word meaning "to be jealous or zealous." The Zealots wanted to be like the Old Testament people, like Phinehas and Elijah, who in their zeal for God's law killed those who led Israel to disobey God's law. The Maccabees who revolted and killed the officers of Antiochus IV were their heroes.

The Zealots arose later than the other groups—during the Roman period. To them, fighting against Rome was in the tradition of their religion. They refused to pay taxes or in any way show loyalty to the Roman rulers.

Throughout the time that the Romans occupied Israel, the Zealots were responsible for assassinations of Roman officials and for small uprisings against the Romans. They could be compared to terrorist groups today, though, of course, they did not have the powerful weapons that some terrorist groups today have.

10 — — — ➤ Discovery at Qumran

Late in 1946 three shepherds were tending their sheep in the area of Qumran. One of the shepherds, Jum a Muhammad Khalil, was amusing himself by tossing rocks at one of the cave openings in the cliff. One rock shattered something inside the cave. Two days later one of the other shepherds, Muhammad Ahmed el-Hamad, squeezed into the cave before his companions woke up. He discovered several clay jars containing scrolls wrapped in linen. These scrolls turned out to be manuscripts from the time of the Essene community. The dry desert air had preserved them for hundreds of years. Do you suppose that God's hand was guiding the rock that crashed into the cave?

Replica of a Dead Sea scroll jar and lid.

More Manuscripts

Cave explorers uncovered more manuscripts, probably the remains of the library of the Essene community. In all, there were 11 caves that provided over 100 scrolls or fragments. These are called the Dead Sea Scrolls. Most of the scrolls are made of leather sheets that were sewn together. The scrolls were handwritten, but they almost looked printed. Margins, columns, and lines were all carefully measured. Sometimes words are missing, but they are written in the margins as though they were added later.

An Important Find

Why are these manuscripts so important? First of all, the Qumran manuscripts are probably the version of the Old Testament closest to the original. They are nearly 1,000 years older than any copies people had before 1946. Second, some of the writings found at Qumran throw light on Jewish life

Looking down into Cave IV.

shortly before and even during the time that Jesus lived in Palestine. Third, the Dead Sea Scrolls give us valuable information about the Qumran community—how the people lived and what they believed.

What Happened to the Scrolls?

At first no one realized the importance of the Dead Sea Scrolls. The shepherds sold four of the scrolls for about $100 to Athanasius Yeshua Samuel, the head of a Syrian Orthodox monastery. In 1954 he tried to sell them through a *Wall Street Journal* advertisement. Eventually the Israeli government bought all of the scrolls and stored them in the Shrine of the Book, a special building in Jerusalem.

The First Seven Scrolls

Here is a brief description of the first seven scrolls found.

- **Two Copies of the Book of Isaiah.** One is a complete scroll, 24 feet long; the other is an incomplete text.

- **Manual of Discipline.** This scroll could be called the constitution of the Qumran community. It gives the rules and responsibilities of community life and explains how new members were admitted. It also includes the beliefs of the Essenes.

- **Commentary on the Book of Habakkuk.** The author of this scroll commented on the Old Testament prophecy of Habakkuk, tying it in to the problems of his own day. It also talks about the Teacher of Righteousness, who was a leader (perhaps the founder) of the community.

- **The Genesis Apocryphon.** This is a collection of first-person stories about some biblical patriarchs of Genesis: Lamech, Enoch, Noah, Abraham, and Sarah.

- **The Scroll of the War of the Sons of Light against the Sons of Darkness.** This is an unusual writing that gives many details about warfare at that time. It pictures the final battle between good and evil.

- **Thanksgiving Hymns.** This book of hymns is very much like the psalms. They were probably written for the use of the community.

Essenes' Beliefs

The Dead Sea Scrolls make it clear that the Essenes believed themselves to be the last of the faithful remnant of God's people. They believed that they alone lived by the true interpretation of the law.

They looked forward to the day of the Lord to bring the messianic age when there would be a new Jerusalem and a new temple. In the new temple pure priests would sacrifice according to God's law, unlike the priests in Jerusalem. Further, the Essenes expected that on the day of the Lord a prophet would come and then two messiahs—a high priest and a king.

In some ways the Essenes at Qumran were close to the truth about the messiah. Both Jesus and the Qumran community recognized many evils in Jewish religious life. But they set about fixing them in very different ways.

Unit 10
The Setting of Christ's Ministry

1 - - - - - - → Bible Memory

❧ ❧

Your love, O Lord, reaches to the heavens,
    your faithfulness to the skies.
Your righteousness is like the mighty mountains,
    your justice like the great deep.
O Lord, you preserve both man and beast.
    How priceless is your unfailing love!
Both high and low among men
    find refuge in the shadow of your wings.
They feast on the abundance of your house;
    you give them drink from your river of delights.
For with you is the fountain of life;
    in your light we see light.

Psalm 36:5–9

❧ ❧

In the beginning was the Word, and the Word was with God, and the Word was God. He was with God in the beginning.

Through him all things were made; without him nothing was made that has been made. In him was life, and that life was the light of men. The light shines in the darkness, but the darkness has not understood it.

The Word became flesh and made his dwelling among us. We have seen his glory, the glory of the One and Only, who came from the Father, full of grace and truth.

—John 1:1–5, 14

2 ━ ━ ━ ━ ━ ➤ Herod the Great

Jesus lived such a long time ago that it is difficult to imagine what it might have been like when he was young. Who was running the government? Where did his family worship? What kind of holidays did they celebrate? What was the land like? In this unit we'll be answering questions like these, and we'll be creating a picture of Jesus' childhood in Palestine.

In this lesson we'll look at the powerful people controlling Palestine, especially the governor, Herod. As we have seen, Rome was now the leading world power. Pompey, Julius Caesar's general, had taken advantage of the quarreling of two Hasmoneans and conquered Judea for Rome. Since Caesar lived in Rome, about 2,000 miles away, he had to choose someone to rule Palestine for him.

How did Herod, an Edomite (Idumean) manage to get the job? For one thing, he had good family connections. His father was a friend of Caesar. When Caesar made Herod's father governor in Judea, Herod got Galilee, one of the four regions of Judea. Idumea was in the south, then Judea, then

Samaria, and then Galilee. Usually a different governor would rule each area, but Herod gained control over all these provinces.

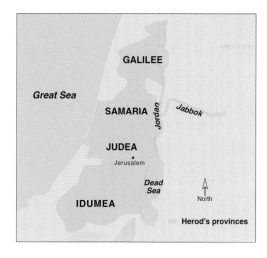

How did Herod become so great and powerful? Three aspects of his character explain his success. For one thing, he was a gifted diplomat. He also had big dreams and the ability to make his dreams a reality. In addition, Herod was extremely suspicious and was always quick to eliminate possible opposition.

Herod and the Sanhedrin

Herod showed his diplomatic skills in the way he handled local government. He knew that managing the cantankerous Jews was one of the keys to political success in Palestine. So Herod allowed the existing Sanhedrin to manage local political and religious affairs for him. These leaders consulted with Herod, and once in a while they reported to Roman governors such as Pontius Pilate. In Jesus' day the Sanhedrin at Jerusalem controlled local affairs and activities throughout Judea.

Three powerful groups held membership in the Sanhedrin. One group was the elders. They were aristocratic, non-priestly heads of tribes and families. Ever since the time of Ezra and Nehemiah there had been groups of elders to guide the religious and political affairs of the Jews. By the time of the period of forced Hellenization, synagogues had popped up in towns throughout the empire. They became places where the elders organized Jewish community life around the law of God. Each synagogue had a council of elders. In the smaller towns there might be 7 elders on the council, but larger towns might have up to 23 elders.

Two other groups were represented on the Sanhedrin, chief priests and teachers of the law. Chief priests were leaders of aristocratic, priestly families. They were wealthy Sadducees, who were eager to cooperate with the Romans. The head of the ruling priestly family held the highest position in the Sanhedrin, that of high priest. The teachers of the law were Pharisees who taught the law of God and its interpretation.

Herod the Clever Diplomat

Herod was also an expert in the diplomatic art of managing international relations. He won the favor of several Roman emperors and was able to maintain his power and influence in Palestine for more than 30 years. Herod always found a way to be on the winning side in the Roman power struggles. Through careful wheeling and dealing, he was given the title "King of the Jews." By 37 B.C. Herod had gained control of Samaria and Judea.

Herod needed all of his diplomatic skills to control the people of Judea and Jerusalem. The Jews living there still hated their distant relatives, the Edomites. Because Herod was an Edomite and the King of Idumea, the Jews mistrusted him. To win their loyalty Herod used an ancient diplomatic ploy. He allied himself with the Jews by marrying Mariamne, a descendant of the Maccabees. Through this marriage Herod hoped to win favor with the Jews and to strengthen his claim to the throne.

Another diplomatic move won favor with many Jews. Herod rebuilt the temple. By 20 B.C. the temple was too small to accommodate all the residents of Jerusalem. The 80,000 to 100,000 pilgrims who came to the temple for special feasts made the crowding even worse. Herod's splendid temple rivaled Solomon's temple in every way except for one thing: Solomon wanted a place of worship that would honor God's majesty and power, but Herod built the temple as part of his political strategy and also as part of his vision for Palestine to honor himself. The temple project wasn't completed until A.D. 64, and the Romans destroyed it in A.D. 70.

Herod the Builder of Monuments

Herod dreamed of a kingdom with buildings as splendid as those in Greece and Rome. He spent much of his 33-year reign beautifying Palestine and building monuments to himself. In addition to the magnificent temple in Jerusalem Herod constructed theaters, stadiums, and fortresses throughout his kingdom. Always the smooth politician, Herod rebuilt Samaria and renamed it in honor of the emperor. He also turned a tiny fishing village on the Mediterranean coast into a major Roman seaport and —you guessed it—

Ruins of a temple in Caesarea built by Herod in honor of Caesar Augustus.

named it Caesarea in honor of Caesar Augustus.

Caesarea was famous for its splendid public buildings and for another great engineering triumph, the water aqueduct. It brought fresh water from Mount Carmel to the city. Almost six miles of the aqueduct had to be dug through limestone. Herod's subjects must have been awed. He counted on their gratitude as well.

For his own security Herod built fortresses. His most famous fortress was Masada, a huge rock with sheer cliffs. It was located in the wilderness near the Dead Sea. Masada also doubled as a resort for Herod and his family. He built a luxurious palace there complete with hot and cold baths, steam rooms, swimming pools, and shady terraces to catch the cool evening breezes. In huge storerooms and water cisterns, Herod kept enough food and water to last for several years—just in case his enemies laid siege.

Aerial view of Masada.

Herod the Suspicious Tyrant

Herod probably wanted to be remembered for his grand building projects. But it's likely that he is better remembered for his violent, cruel suppression of those who opposed him and of those he imagined were plotting against him. In the tradition of tyrants, he killed off the opposition. Mariamne's grandfather was a powerful high priest in Jerusalem. Herod had him killed. Mariamne's brother died under suspicious circumstances. When he was called to Egypt to account for the incident, Herod ordered Mariamne killed if he didn't return alive.

Herod gave the same orders when he left Jerusalem on another occasion. When Mariamne protested furiously, he had her killed. Next Herod killed her mother, Alexandra. The murders didn't end with her mother. Herod killed Mariamne's two sons. Then he imprisoned and executed yet another son. You can imagine Herod's response when the wise men from the east came to inquire about the newborn King of the Jews. Do you remember what happened to Bethlehem's innocent baby boys?

Herod's hippodrome, an open-air stadium.

3 — ➡ A Journey through Palestine

Palestine is an unusual land. Its geography and climate are extremely varied, even though it is only about 8,019 square miles large. It's about the size of the state of New Jersey and about twice the size of Nova Scotia's Cape Breton Island. There are five longitudinal land regions. Look at the map of the land regions. There is dry, hot desert near the Dead Sea in the south and snow on the slopes of Mount Hermon in the north. There is good, flat farmland along the Mediterranean Sea and Jordan River, but much of the country is hilly, rocky, and barren. In this lesson, we'll take a tour of Palestine and visit historical places of Old Testament times.

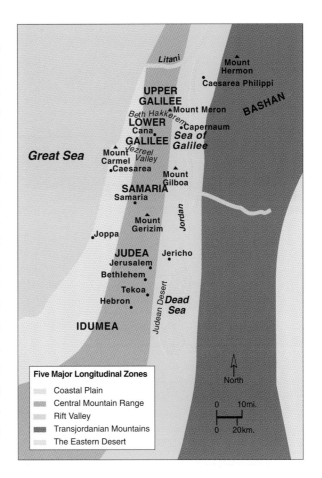

Five Major Longitudinal Zones
- Coastal Plain
- Central Mountain Range
- Rift Valley
- Transjordanian Mountains
- The Eastern Desert

The Northeastern Region

Let's begin in the area north and east of the Sea of Galilee. In Bible times this region was called Bashan; today it's known as the Golan Heights. This northern area was known for its cattle and its mighty oaks. In the days of the Roman Empire, Bashan was an important wheat-producing region. This northern area gets the most rain in Palestine, about 30–60 inches a year. It has many small lakes, swamps, and streams.

Mount Hermon.

With an elevation of over 9,000 feet, Mount Hermon's snow-covered peak towers over this northernmost area. Mount Hermon was the location for several important events. For example, Peter made his confession that Jesus was the Christ at Caesarea Philippi, which is located at the base of Mount Hermon. Jesus' transfiguration probably took place somewhere on Mount Hermon.

Galilee

As we travel west and slightly south from Mount Hermon, we enter the region called Galilee. The northern part is called Upper Galilee. It extends from the region around the Litani River in the north to the Beth Hakkerem Valley in the south. Around Mount Meron the elevation reaches nearly 4,000 feet. Although the elevation is high, the soil is fertile.

From the south in the Jezreel Valley looking at Nazareth in the hills.

Lower Galilee extends to the Jezreel Valley on the south. In Lower Galilee none of the hills are over 2,000 feet high. However, there are steep hills and cliffs here. For example, Christ's hometown of Nazareth has a cliff on the southwest side of town.

The Sea of Galilee is in this area. Actually, it's a lake that's about 15 miles long and 6 miles wide. Jesus chose some disciples from among fishermen on this lake. Jesus also performed his first miracle in the Galilean city of Cana. And Capernaum, which is on the northern coast of the Sea of Galilee, became the center for much of his preaching.

The Sea of Galilee at the southwest end.

Samaria

The region of Samaria is south of the Valley of Jezreel. This land is full of hills, steep ridges, and deep ravines. Usually the Jews crossed the Jordan River and traveled along its east banks to avoid this dangerous, rugged region. The Jews also avoided this region because of the hatred between Jews and Samaritans.

Our first Samaritan stop is the famous seaport of Caesarea. It began as a small fishing village called Strato's Tower. A little south of here is Joppa, another seaport. This Samaritan city was important to two famous preach-

Caesarea.

Joppa.

ers. You can't forget Jonah, who jumped on a ship in Joppa to try to run away from his preaching assignment to the people in Nineveh. Centuries later the apostle Peter rested on a Joppa rooftop and received a vision that convinced him to preach to the Gentiles.

In the heart of Samaria is the capital city, Samaria. Do you remember the infamous queen who taunted Elijah there? Not far away is Mount Gerizim. Near Mount Gerizim the tribes of Judah recited the curses and covenant blessings after they entered Canaan. Experts also believe that God commanded Abraham to sacrifice Isaac on this mountain.

Judea and the Judean Wilderness

Jerusalem from the north.

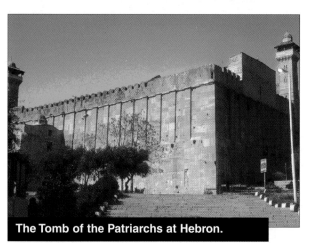
The Tomb of the Patriarchs at Hebron.

As we approach Jerusalem from the north, we can see the hills in the distance; their tops look down on the city. Deep ravines protect Jerusalem on three sides—all but the north. That's one reason David chose this place for his capital city—it was easy to defend.

The hill country of Judea is from 10–14 miles wide and extends about 40 miles south from Jerusalem. The hills of Judea are higher than those of Samaria, and the only way to travel from north to south is along the road at the top of the ridge.

If we followed the ridge route and traveled south from Jerusalem, we would come to Hebron. Here the mountains rise to an elevation of over

3,000 feet, and here the main ridge route and two major branches came together. David choose Hebron as his first headquarters because of its strategic location. The location also made Hebron a commercial city. On market day farmers from the Judean hills brought their olives, grapes, and pomegranates to town. They traded with Bedouins from the south for sheep, donkeys, camels, and leather goods.

We won't stay in Hebron long because we're going to visit the Judean wilderness. Pack your water bottles and make sure you wear a hat! We'll turn directly east to make the descent to the wilderness. This descent is pretty dramatic. In a matter of 10 miles we go down 4,300 feet (l310 m.) The air is getting hotter and drier. Water is harder to find. Thirst becomes a problem! We're in a desert, the wilderness of Judea, where Jesus was tempted by Satan and where David fled from Saul.

The Judean wilderness.

The Dead Sea

It isn't long until we can see the Dead Sea in the distance. To get there we have to go downhill all the way. The Dead Sea is the lowest spot in the

world, about 1,300 feet below sea level. But the Dead Sea doesn't help our thirst at all. The water isn't good. Nothing lives in it. It's got potassium, sulfur, chloride, and other minerals in it, along with lots of salt. In fact, another name for it was the Salt Sea. If you decide to swim in it, you will float like a cork.

The Dead Sea and Jordan Valley as seen from the top of Herodium, the fortress of Herod Antipas.

Salt was not the only product gathered from the Dead Sea. Ancient people collected floating clumps of a sticky, black petroleum substance called bitumen. Josephus said that this gooey substance looked like the heads of decapitated bulls. Bitumen must have had a tar-like quality, because it was used to caulk ships. Because of the bitumen, some ancient writers called the sea Lake Asphaltitis.

Herod's aqueduct.

As we head north towards Jericho we can see an old aqueduct built by Herod the Great, which brings water from the hills around Jerusalem and down to Jericho. After stopping at Jericho, we travel up to Jerusalem again. It's a winding road through the hills. It's easy to see why this road was a dangerous trip in the days of Jesus. There are many places for robbers to hide to make surprise attacks and then quickly disappear again.

After a short time of sightseeing we leave Jerusalem and head out into the hill country toward the small town of Bethlehem, Jesus birthplace. We might see a few vineyards along the way. But we will certainly see sheep and goats nibbling on grass and weeds in this rocky, dry countryside. We'll also see shepherds keeping watch over the flocks. Not far from Bethlehem is the town of Tekoa. It was the hometown of Amos, the sheep farmer turned prophet.

Looking back at Jerusalem from the Bethlehem-Jerusalem highway.

The Shephelah and the Coastal Plain

As we travel west, the journey gets easier; the hills are not as steep. These are the shephelah, which means "low hills." These gently rolling hills are good farmland that receives a good supply of rain. In Old Testament days the Israelites fought many battles with the Philistines over this fertile territory.

Finally the hills descend to flat, fertile farmland that gets plenty of moisture from the Mediterranean Sea. This is the coastal plain. The far north and the south of this plain were hardly ever a part of Israel's territory. In Old Testament times this plain belonged to the Philistines in the south and the Phoenicians in the north.

The Judean foothills, the shephelah.

At the Lebanese-Israeli border looking south into Israel's coastal plain.

The Valley of Jezreel

Heading north and a bit inland we come to the Jezreel Valley, which is situated between Samaria and Galilee. Mount Carmel blocked easy land travel along the Mediterranean, so people went through the Jezreel Valley to get around it. It was in the rugged region of Mount Carmel that Elijah defeated the priests of Baal. The Jezreel Valley is fertile; there is much rain-

The Jezreel Valley, with Megiddo to the right of center, Mount Tabor across the way, and Nazareth to the left.

fall, good soil, and flat land. Because of this flatness, it was also a good route to take from west to east. In Old Testament times a person could get rich by controlling this important transportation route. The famous judges Deborah and Gideon won great victories along this valley. And the Philistines chased Saul out of this valley onto Mount Gilboa, where he killed himself before they could capture him.

We've made a long trip. Imagine walking over the land, over the dusty paths and hard rocks in sandals! That's the way Jesus and his disciples probably traveled. No wonder people in Bible times had the custom of foot-washing. Parts of Palestine are productive, and other parts are barren desert. In fact, Palestine has all the major climates of the world except arctic tundra and tropical rain forest. When we read the Bible stories, knowing where they took place in Palestine will help us understand the stories themselves.

4 — ➤ Judaism at the Time of Christ

By the time that Jesus was born, Jewish religious life was significantly different from the practices in the days of Moses. The exile and the influence of Hellenism had changed Jewish understanding of God's requirements. In this lesson we will examine some of the changes in Judaism. We'll also look at their religious beliefs and hopes.

One God

One of the main things that defined Judaism and made it so different from other religions was the belief that there is only one God. The name for this belief is monotheism. The Israelites believed in one God, the Creator, who cared for the earth and loved the people he had formed in his own image. If they loved and trusted this one creator God, they did not need to live in fear of unpredictable gods or strange events in the natural world.

The Israelites lived among the Canaanites who were polytheists, people who believed in more than one god. You remember that God repeatedly told the people to stay away from Baal, Asherah, and other Canaanite gods. The Canaanites did not know that one God had created the earth and all of its natural rhythms. They were often fearful and worried about pleasing their gods because displeased gods would send famine and death.

Hear, O Israel: The Lord our God, the Lord is one.
Love the Lord your God with all your heart and with all your soul and with all your strength.

Deuteronomy 6:4–5

To constantly remind themselves of the one God, Jewish children memorized and repeated Deuteronomy 6:4–5 every day. These verses are known as the Shema. Part of the Shema reinforced their understanding and belief in one God: "Hear, O Israel: the Lord our God, the Lord is one." Their response to this loving God was not one of fear. They were told to "Love the Lord your God."

The Torah

Obedience to the law of God was always an important part of Jewish religious practice. In fact, the Torah—the law—was the very heart of Jewish religion. From the earliest times the prophets called the people to be obedient to the law of God. Their obedience was not to be out of fear but because obedience made life good. It led to faithful worship at the temple and healthy human relationships.

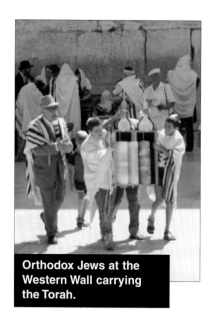

Orthodox Jews at the Western Wall carrying the Torah.

During the time of exile the Jews came to realize that their captivity was a punishment for their disobedience to God's law. In the years that followed, the Jewish religion began to put more and more stress on the importance of keeping the law to please the Lord. The forceful reaction against Hellenism gave the law a further push toward the center of Jewish religious life. Fervent devotion to the law was seen as a way to keep out Hellenistic religious practices.

As we saw in the last unit, obeying the law became so important that some Jews added laws to the ones God had given them. These additional laws were intended to help the people apply God's laws to every situation in their lives. This was good. But in Jesus' day many Jews, especially the Pharisees, taught that these human laws were equal with God's laws. This was not good. Trying to keep all of these laws became a burden to the people instead of the delight that the psalmists talked about. It seemed that the people forgot that the basic commandment was to love God. They lived in fear that they would anger God—and the Pharisees—by breaking one of the hundreds of manmade commandments.

For example, according to the oral tradition it was unlawful to heal someone on the Sabbath day unless his or her life was in danger. One day when Jesus healed on the Sabbath, the Pharisees accused him of breaking the law. But they didn't seem to think that it was wrong to plot on the Sabbath to kill Jesus.

This incident points up another problem. To some Jews, especially the Pharisees, obeying the law had become an outward exercise. They didn't seem to grasp that God wanted them to obey the law from their hearts. Jesus had many conflicts with Jews concerning the law. But Jesus didn't throw out the law of God. He was reacting against their misunderstanding and misuse of God's law.

The Torah

If you come across the word *Pentateuch*, you should know that it refers to the first five books of our Old Testament. It also refers to the same books found in Hebrew Scriptures. The name Pentateuch contains the prefix *penta*, which means "five." Another name for these books is "The Five Books of Moses." The Torah is a third name for these books. The word *Torah* means "law or instruction." Sometimes the word *Torah* is used to include the oral tradition as well as the written laws.

The Messiah

During and after the exile, the Jews hoped for a messiah, an "anointed one." Remember how some of the Old Testament prophets spoke about the messiah as they described the glorious future that God had in store for his people? Isaiah, Ezekiel, and Zechariah were three prophets who especially talked about him.

However, through the years, many different ideas about this messiah developed. For example, the Essenes of the Qumran community were waiting for two or three messiahs. Some Jews believed that the messiah would be a great priest; others insisted that he would be a king.

Jewish hope that a messiah would come to deliver them soared during the Hasmonean period when the Jews won their independence. But because the priests who ruled the Jews during this period were unfaithful and selfish, many Jews gave up the idea of a messiah-priest. During this time, the hope for a messiah-king grew. Their hopes were dashed when the Romans took over Palestine.

Then the hope began to grow again. By the time Jesus was born, most Jews shared the belief that the messiah was coming soon. This is what they believed about him:

- He would be a mighty warrior of David's line.
- He would be a human king who would be a champion for his people.
- He would rely on God.

- His kingdom would be an earthly kingdom with Jerusalem at its center.
- His greatest task would be the destruction of God's enemies. In Christ's time this meant deliverance from Roman oppression.

The Temple

The temple was still an important part of the Jewish religion when Jesus was born, but it was not the center of religion as it had been in the days of Solomon. There were several reasons for this. First, during the Persian period (perhaps as early as the exile) synagogues sprang up. They gradually became religious centers. Second, as we've seen, the law became increasingly important. Third, the priests during the Hasmonean period were so corrupt that many people turned away from the temple. Fourth, the unpopular Sadducees were in control of the temple services.

However, the temple was still a special place. Only at the temple could sacrifices be offered to atone for sin. But sacrificing to pay the price for sin was no longer as important as in the early days. And the priests made it hard for the people to find atonement for their sins. The people had to pay taxes for the upkeep of the temple and for the priests' support. This tax was in addition to the already heavy taxes the people paid to the Romans. People traveling from far places were also forced to buy over-priced animals for sacrifice.

5 ▬ ▬ ▬ ➤ Special Days and Feasts

There are not many people in North America who cannot name at least one Christmas tradition. Festivals and holidays tell us a lot about a group of people, their history and their values. Some national holidays celebrate victories in war while others are solemn and serious. Traditional Jewish holidays contain both aspects. They are both joyful and solemn.

Jewish celebrations seem foreign to most Christians. Yet Jesus celebrated them with great enthusiasm, and he used the symbols of these feasts to explain who he was. As you read about Jewish feasts and festivals, try to think of ways that Jesus might have used the festivals to reveal his mission on earth.

To get started, think about this example. Water was a symbol used for the Feast of Tabernacles. During this feast, water from the Pool of Siloam was poured out. This action symbolized the way that God had provided water for his people during the 40 years in the desert. Do you know what Jesus said about the water he would give?

In this lesson you will read about several Jewish festivals. You will also discover some ways that Jesus used the festivals to show the people who he really was.

The Sabbath

The Sabbath was the seventh day of the Hebrew week. It began at sunset on Friday night and ended at sunset the following day. It was a day of rest for everyone—even for slaves and animals. The Jews observed this special day every week to celebrate God's creation of the world and his saving acts during the exodus from Egypt.

Passover and Feast of Unleavened Bread

The Jews celebrated seven major festivals. Five of these were instituted by God through Moses; two were added later. The most important festival was probably Passover and the Feast of Unleavened Bread, celebrated during the Jewish month of Nisan. Nisan coincides with our calendar's end of March and beginning of April. Passover was one of the

Orthodox Jews at the Western Wall during Passover week.

three great pilgrim festivals, a festival that drew Jews from all over to Jerusalem. Passover commemorated the night in Egypt when the angel of death passed over the houses of the Jews who had obeyed the instructions of Moses. The firstborn sons of these homes would not have to die; the blood of a lamb sprinkled on the doorpost saved them.

As part of the eight-day Passover celebration, Jews also observed the Feast of Unleavened Bread. This feast recalled the night that the Israelites left Egypt. They left in such a hurry that they didn't have time to put yeast in the bread dough. During Passover and the following week Jews ate bread without yeast (unleavened bread) to remember this night when God delivered them from Egypt.

When Jesus was 12 years old, he went with his parents to Jerusalem to celebrate Passover. Passover was also the feast that Jesus celebrated with his disciples on the night that he was arrested.

Feast of Weeks/Pentecost

Fifty days after Passover the Jews celebrated a second great festival. Pilgrims traveled back to Jerusalem, this time to give God thanks for the harvest of grain. The Old Testament name for this festival was the Feast of Weeks, but in the New Testament it was known as Pentecost (from the Greek word for fiftieth). On the Jewish calendar this feast was held in the month of Sivan, which coincides with the later part of May on our calendar. At Pentecost the people gave God loaves of bread made from their harvested grain, as well as animal sacrifices (Leviticus 23:15–22).

Pentecost from the **Book of Hours**.

It was on Pentecost, 50 days after Easter, that the Holy Spirit came upon the Christians gathered in Jerusalem. It was a fitting day, for these Christians represented the first harvest of believers.

Feast of Trumpets/Rosh Hashanah

The next festival was a one-day celebration occurring on the first day of the seventh month, Tishri, which coincides with September on our calendar. This was a special Sabbath day, for on this day the people remembered that God instituted the Sabbath. The priest would stand on the pinnacle of the temple and blow a ram's horn from morning to evening. No work was done, and special sacrifices were offered. In Nehemiah's time this festival became the New Year's Day celebration, Rosh Hashanah. It was also a time of self-examination. In Palestine this is when the new year begins for the farmers; the rains fall and soften the soil for the plow.

Stone carving showing a menorah, shofar, and incense shovel.

Yom Kippur

The tenth day of Tishri was a solemn day of repentance—the Day of Atonement or Yom Kippur. On this day all Israel confessed, mourned for its sins, and asked God for forgiveness. The priests offered special sacrifices to cleanse the temple, themselves, and the people. On this day the priests chose two goats. One was sacrificed, and the high priest sprinkled some of its blood in the Most Holy Place. This was the only day of the year that the high priest entered the Most Holy Place. The other goat, which was called the scapegoat, was driven out into the wilderness; it carried the sins of the people away with it.

Feast of Tabernacles

Jews celebrated the third great pilgrim festival, the Feast of Tabernacles (Feast of Booths) from the 15th to the 21st of Tishri. The people spent these days camping in tents (tabernacles) or in booths made of branches. The feast reminded them of God's protection and his provision of food and water during their wilderness journey. Since this festival also celebrated the gathering of the harvest, it was sometimes called the Feast of Ingathering. During this time the people also went to the temple for animal sacrifices and grain offerings.

The Feast of Dedication and Purim

The last two annual feasts had their beginning after the exile. The Feast of Dedication was celebrated during the Jewish month of Kislev. This festival is also known as Hanukkah or the Festival of Lights. It reminded the Jews of the cleansing and rededication of the temple in 164 B.C. by Judas Maccabeus and his followers after it had been defiled by Antiochus Epiphanes and the provision of oil for the temple lamps. The Jews celebrated with daily lighting of lamps, singing, processions, and temple sacrifices.

Purim was a two-day feast during the Jewish month of Adar (February/March). This festival celebrated the victory of the Persian Jews over their enemies through Esther's bravery. "Purim" means "lot"; Haman cast lots to decide when the Jews should be massacred. The Book of Esther was publicly read. The people gave alms and enjoyed good food and drink.

6 ━ ━ ━ ━ ➡ The Light Will Come

Bible Reference: Luke 1:5–25, 57–80

Have you ever noticed that when it is dark and cloudy the colors of grass, trees, and flowers seem much duller than when the sun shines on them? Have you ever noticed that when you wake up in a bad mood everything seems to bother you? When we walk in shadows, everything seems dull and lifeless.

The Setting

After the exiles returned from Babylon, the sun may have been shining in Palestine. But for God's people, it must have seemed like there was a permanent cloud cover. God was giving them the silent treatment; the prophets weren't talking. Many Jews acted more like sophisticated Greeks than like God's faithful people. The Roman rulers were tyrants, and King Herod was a beast. Their religious leaders competed for positions of power and prestige, and they often ignored true religion. Meanwhile, the violent Zealots attracted hot-blooded young Jews with promises of revolution. The situation was about as gloomy as it could get.

The Characters

But God had not forgotten his people or his covenant promises. He was moving behind the scenes to break through the clouds with an astonishing light. In today's lesson we'll see how God used Zechariah and Elizabeth in his plan to turn on the light. This faithful old Jewish couple lived under a shadow made deeper and darker by their own private pain. They could not have children. Each day they carried a burden of disgrace because childlessness was seen as a sign of God's disfavor.

Yet in spite of their personal grief, they obeyed God's commands. Zechariah was a faithful priest, and Elizabeth was also a descendant of

Aaron. Twice a year Zechariah served for a week at the temple in Jerusalem. One day Zechariah journeyed to Jerusalem to do his priestly work, leaving Elizabeth behind in their village.

Zechariah was probably surprised and pleased this time when the lot was cast and he was chosen to offer incense. It was a solemn, once-in-a-lifetime honor to burn incense in the temple. When the smoke from the incense floated up and over the worshipers, they would fall down, and their prayers would rise like the smoke.

Zechariah Asking for a Writing Tablet (19th century engraving).

As Zechariah was busy burning incense, God interrupted to make a special birth announcement. As you read the story, notice the different ways that Zechariah and Elizabeth responded. Watch also for the way that their sadness turned into delight and Zechariah's doubt turned into praise.

7 - ➤ Mary, God's Unexpected Choice

Bible Reference: Luke 1:26–56

Just a few months after announcing the birth of John the Baptist, Gabriel appeared to Mary with another astonishing message.

Can you imagine an angel tapping you on the shoulder and saying, "I don't want to startle you, but you are going to be a parent very soon. And by the way, it will be a miracle." Well, that's just what happened to Mary. Read **Jewish Marriage Customs** to find out why his message may have been a bit troubling to Mary.

Do you ever wonder exactly what Mary was like? Was she quiet and shy? Did she want to laugh with her friends instead of helping her mother in the house? Although we don't know much about Mary's personality, we do know that she was not from an educated or powerful family. As a poor woman, she

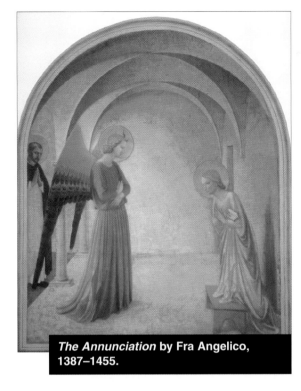

The Annunciation by Fra Angelico, 1387–1455.

would never have dreamed of being someone special.

Although she was uneducated, Mary's response to God's call was amazing. At first she was fearful, then accepting. It wasn't long before she was filled with delight, and she prayed one of the loveliest songs of praise in the whole Bible.

Jewish Marriage Customs

Being engaged was a big deal during Jesus' time. An engagement then was more permanent than many marriages today. The only way to break an engagement was through divorce. But women had no legal right to divorce. Only men were allowed to divorce sexually unfaithful partners. As a matter of fact, men were allowed to publicly accuse their wives of being unfaithful. If a woman was found guilty, she could be stoned to death. No wonder Mary was troubled.

The Holy Spirit must have been extra busy, because Mary had a surprisingly clear understanding of her son's mission. She knew that proud Jewish leaders were in for a big surprise. The messiah would build his kingdom in the hearts of the poor and humble. God was going to use a peasant girl from the little town of Nazareth to fulfill his glorious promise to make all things right and to make us all insiders.

8 ------➤ The Birth of Jesus

Bible Reference: Luke 2:1–20

Jesus' family was ready for his birth. Mary felt deep joy over the coming birth of her son. Mary's cousin Elizabeth understood the significance of the holy child. And because of Gabriel's heavenly encouragement, Joseph was at peace with his fiancée's pregnancy. Most of God's people didn't realize it, but the deepest longings and the wildest hopes of Old Testament believers were going to be fulfilled. The incarnation was about to materialize.

The Incarnation

The word *incarnation* sounds formal, but its meaning is pretty earthy. The root of incarnation is the Latin word that means flesh. God took on flesh and blood to become like us. Why did it have to happen?

God created all of us in his image. Every evening God came to the garden to walk with Adam and Eve. He knew and understood them perfectly. Adam and Eve must have been perfectly at ease asking God questions about their beautiful world. But after sin came to the world, they couldn't talk openly with God anymore, and they had a hard time trusting each other. God's presence terrified them. Since then anger, suspicion, and hate have plagued all human relationships.

God wasn't happy with the situation, and neither were Adam and Eve. So God made a plan to bring back the perfect peace they had experienced in the garden. To bridge the gap between God and humans, God joined heaven and earth in Jesus. The perfect Son of God became human, taking on flesh and our human form. In Ephesians 2:14 Paul said, "For he himself [Jesus] is our peace, who has made the two one and has destroyed the barrier, the dividing wall of hostility."

The Message of the Angels

The angels sang of this healing peace, not to the Jewish leaders but to the shepherds who guarded the sheep at night. The peace the angels announced was of cosmic importance. Jesus was going to repair earth's connection with heaven. The angels knew that one day human creatures would again walk and talk with God. They knew that one day people would no longer fight and quarrel with each other. And they assured the poor shepherds that there was room in God's family for anyone with a humble heart.

The Nativity by Correggio, 1530.

The peace that the angels sang about was not what many Jewish people expected. They wanted to kick the Romans out of Palestine. Yet the Romans helped fulfill Micah's prophecy of a coming Prince of Peace. Here's how it happened. Micah 5:2 says, "But you, Bethlehem Ephrathah . . . out of you will come for me one who will be ruler over Israel." The prophecy meant that the messiah would be born in Bethlehem, but we know that Mary and Joseph lived in Nazareth. Thanks to the Roman census Mary and Joseph, along with everyone else, had to travel to the hometown of their ancestors. Joseph was from the family of King David, who came from Bethlehem. It must have been inconvenient and incredibly tiring for Mary to make the three-day journey from Nazareth to Bethlehem. Her baby was due at any time. But she and Joseph made it to Bethlehem, and Jesus was born there—just as the prophet had predicted.

9 ▬ ▬ ➤ Baby Jesus in the Temple

Bible Reference: Luke 2:21–40

What's in a Name?

Do you ever wonder what it was like when you were born? What did your mother think when she first laid eyes on you? Do you ever wonder what your parents were thinking when they chose your name? Where did it come from—a movie star, an athlete, a grandparent?

Sometimes parents name a baby after a famous athlete and hope that the hero's abilities will magically transfer to their child. Often the name doesn't really fit. A boy named Kareem may hate basketball and love to cook. People don't always live up to the expectations that come with their names.

When Jesus came, all the expectations for his future were wrapped up in his name, and he had no trouble living up to them. *Jesus* is Greek for the Hebrew name Joshua, and Joshua means "Yahweh is salvation." The name fit perfectly because God had given it to him.

The Law Fulfilled

One expectation was that Jesus would fulfill the requirements of the law. He would be the perfect sacrifice. Luke shows that Mary and Joseph were careful to obey the law. When Jesus was eight days old, Mary and Joseph took Jesus to the temple to be circumcised and named, just as the law required. They also obeyed the law by giving an offering of a pair of pigeons or doves for their firstborn son, just as the Jews had been doing ever since the exodus.

Jesus' Mission Confirmed

The naming ceremony was also significant because two old people recognized Jesus' identity and mission. One of these people was an old man named Simeon. Simeon was "moved by the Spirit" to go to the temple courts at the time Mary and Joseph were there with Jesus. They must have been surprised when old Simeon shuffled up

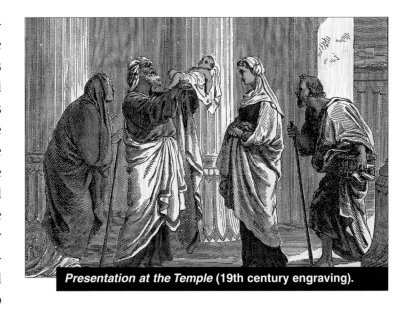

Presentation at the Temple (19th century engraving).

to them and asked to hold their baby. Can you imagine their excitement when he praised God for Jesus, who was the promised Light to the Gentiles. Can you imagine what they thought when he told them that Jesus would be rejected and that Mary's heart would break. You'd think that Simeon's message was enough for them to digest. But then an 84-year-old prophetess named Anna approached them. She too recognized Jesus as the Savior of the world and told everyone around her that the baby Jesus was indeed the Messiah. She knew that his name was a perfect fit.

A Bridge

Anna and Simeon bridge the gap between the Old Testament and the New Testament. They knew the prophecies of the prophets. They knew of God's promise to send the messiah. They both were part of the faithful remnant who were watching and waiting for the messiah to come. God rewarded them and allowed them to see their prayers answered.

Anna and Simeon were not temple priests or teachers of the law. They were ordinary people who recognized Jesus as the Messiah.

10 ━ ━ ━ ━ ━ ➤ Epiphany Eyes

Bible Reference: Matthew 2

For most North Americans, Christmas is over as soon as Christmas Day is finished and the presents are all opened. For many Christians, however, the celebration of Jesus' birth continues all the way to January 6, the feast of the Epiphany. The word *epiphany* means "a revelation." Epiphany celebrates the visit of the Magi to Jesus in Bethlehem. God revealed the Light of the World to these Gentiles with the soft brilliance of a star. God also gave them the eyes to see the marvelous news of the Savior's birth. Their understanding led to reverence, awe, and deep joy.

Who were these strangers from the east? We have all seen Christmas cards picturing three wise men in fine clothing riding camels across a desert with a bright star overhead. All the Bible says is "Magi from the east came to Jerusalem." We have a couple of clues in order to try to understand these mysterious strangers. Matthew calls them *Magi* from a Greek word meaning "magic." People began to use the word during the time of the Medes and Persians of the sixth century B.C. In Persia the Magi were a powerful priestly group. They were experts in medicine, religion, magic, astrology, and astronomy.

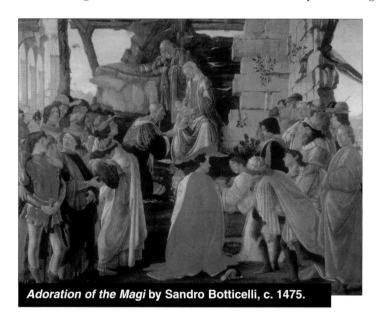
Adoration of the Magi by Sandro Botticelli, c. 1475.

There were others who heard the promise of the messiah but could not see God's love revealed in Jesus the Messiah. Herod was blinded by fear and hatred. The teachers of the law were blinded by their pride. They did not have epiphany eyes.

As you read the story of Herod and the Magi, watch for their responses to the good news of salvation.

Ancient Astrology

According to modern astronomers, in 7 B.C. it looked like the planets Jupiter and Saturn passed by each other three times. This event caught the attention of astrologers, people who figured out people's fate by the position of the stars. The next year something even more exciting occurred—Jupiter  and Saturn were joined by Mars. This massing of planets was extremely rare; it happens only once every 805 years! It occurred in February under the zodiac sign Pisces. Ancient wise men considered Pisces the sign of the House of the Hebrews. Jupiter was the king's planet, and Saturn was the defender of Palestine. The signs then pointed the Magi to Jerusalem to search for the new king of the Jews.

11 – – – – ➤ A Passover Journey

Bible Reference: Luke 2:41–52

Going to School in Nazareth

In Jesus' time Nazareth was just a typical small Jewish village with an open marketplace and a one-story synagogue. The synagogue was also the school. Jesus probably started school when he was six years old. He sat on the ground with the other boys in front of the rabbi to learn his lessons. The rabbi wore a long white tunic covered with a prayer shawl and taught the Torah. Girls did not attend school; they stayed home and learned household skills from their mothers.

Education for Jesus and the other boys centered on the law, the Torah. The rabbi read from a scroll in a rhythmic pattern. The rhythm helped the students memorize more easily. Part of the time the boys sat at one of the long benches along the walls of the synagogue, where they practiced writing Hebrew passages. From the rabbi Jesus learned to love the law and the Jewish festivals.

The Passover Pilgrimage

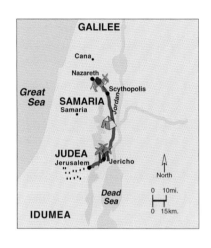

One festival that Jesus' family celebrated each spring was the Passover. This was one of the three "pilgrim feasts" that required the people to travel to Jerusalem. Jesus was 12 years old when his family made the Passover journey recorded in Luke 2. Here's what it was probably like.

At the beginning it's likely that Jesus was eager to help get ready and impatient to get started. He probably helped his father load food and supplies on their donkey for the three- or four-day journey. At the end of the first day Jesus' family may have stopped in the city of Scythopolis. It would have been a safe stopping point because a Roman garrison was stationed there. It was also a good place to meet other pilgrims going to Jerusalem.

The Jordan Valley north of Jericho.

On the second day the pilgrims would head south down the Jordan Valley, a level and easy road to travel. As they walked along, the hills of Samaria were on their right and the hills of Gilead were on their left. Except for a strip along the river, this is a desert region; there are no towns, only an occasional fort. The second night the pilgrims probably slept outside, somewhere along the road.

On the third day the pilgrims arrived and stayed in Jericho. It was a lush oasis, full of palm and date trees. The travelers always looked forward to the Jericho stop.

The fourth day was the hardest part of the journey. The road from Jericho to Jerusalem was not only steep but also rugged and desolate. Here the pilgrims began to sing the psalms of ascent as they went up to the temple of the Lord. Their first glimpse of the splendid gold

Jericho date palm.

and white temple must have been one of the high points of the journey.

The road coming into present-day Jerusalem from the north.

In the Temple

As you read this story about Jesus, try to imagine what Jesus might have thought as he watched the high priest offer the sacrifices required by the law of Moses. What might Jesus have felt when his family gathered to listen to Joseph tell the story of the exodus and the first Passover lamb? What was Jesus' goal as he talked in the temple? What was he trying to tell Mary by his response to her scolding? What did Jesus know about his life's journey?

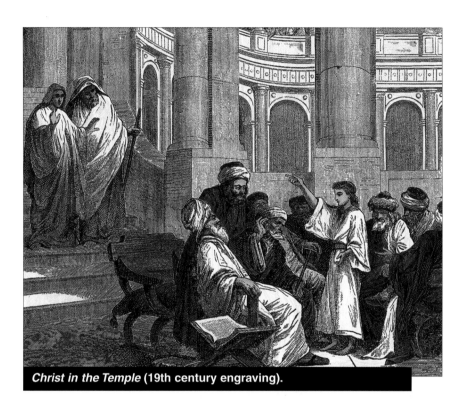

Christ in the Temple (19th century engraving).